D0201054

A COACH FOR ALL SEASONS

To Bruce.

Best Wishes to a great basketball fan. May God bless you in all your endeavors.

Morgan Wootten

Morgan Wootten
and Bill Gilbert

MASTERS PRESS

A Division of Howard W. Sams & Company

Published by Masters Press
A Division of Howard W. Sams & Company
2647 Waterfront Pkwy E. Dr, Suite 100
Indianapolis, IN 46214

© 1997 Morgan Wootten and Bill Gilbert
All rights reserved. Published 1997

Printed in the United States of America.

No part of this publication may be reproduced, stored in
a retrieval system, or transmitted, in any form or by any
means, electronic, mechanical, photocopying, recording,
or otherwise, without the prior permission of Masters
Press.

97 98 99 00 01 02 10 9 8 7 6 5 4 3 2 1

Library of Congress Cataloging-Publication Data

Wootten, Morgan.
    A coach for all seasons / Morgan Wootten and Bill
    Gilbert.
        p.   cm.
    ISBN 1-57028-150-5 (cloth)
    1. Wootten, Morgan. 2. Basketball coaches--United
States--Biography. 3. DeMatha Catholic High School
(Hyattsville, Md.)
I. Gilbert, Bill, 1931- . II. Title.
GV884.W67A32   1997   97-30480
796.323'092--dc21   CIP
[B]

To my donor, Rochelle McCoy,

A world-class wife and mother,

For the continuing gift of life.

And to God, for allowing me to continue as a teacher and a coach.

This book is respectfully and gratefully dedicated

Morgan Wootten
Hyattsville, Maryland
September 1, 1997

Some Special Thank You's

The most fitting way for me to start this book is to say thank you to the many people to whom I owe a special debt of gratitude:

All the outstanding young student-athletes I've had the privilege of teaching and coaching.

My respected colleagues in the teaching and coaching professions.

The members of the Gettysburg, Pennsylvania, Ambulance Service.

The Emergency Room staff at Gettysburg Hospital.

The Penn State Helicopter team.

My magnificent team of doctors — Drs. James Burdick, Paul Thuluvath, Andrew Klein, Ken Chavin, Frank Sanzaro, Stan Silverberg, Donald O'Kieffe, and the entire medical staff at Johns Hopkins University Hospital.

All the wonderful nurses at JHU's medical Intensive Care Unit, Surgical Intensive Care Unit, Intermediate Care Unit and the staff on my floor at JHU — Nelson 7.

My JHU therapists, Chris Downes and Tamerill Faison, and the entire physical therapy staff at Johns Hopkins.

Jeff Wright and his excellent staff at Providence Hospital's Malta Center.

All the members of the news media for their cooperation during my recovery both at the hospital and at home, for their thoroughness and accuracy in reporting my story and for their genuine public service in making the world more aware of the need for organ donors.

All the wonderful people who prayed for me, sent cards and flowers, expressed their concern in so many ways, and sustained me and lifted my spirits.

My donor's family, Ray McCoy, a wonderful husband and father, and his magnificent twins, Randall and Ray, plus Rochelle's parents, Shirley and Charles Mitchell.

My daughter, Cathy, for her many innovative ideas in the preparation of this book.

My Number One Team of all time, our children — Cathy, Carol, Tricia, Brendan and Joe — for their love, loyalty and steadfastness.

And to Kathy, the greatest wife, mother, nurse and friend a man could ever dream of.

Contents

Never give in — never, never, never, never! — in nothing great or small, large or petty — never give in, except to convictions of honor and good sense.

Winston Churchill
on his formula for success, at The Harrow
School Near London,
October 29, 1941.
Quoted often by Morgan
Wootten to his basketball
teams.

People say Morgan Wootten is the best high school basketball coach in the country. I disagree. I know of no finer coach at any level — high school, college or pro. I've said it elsewhere, and I'll say it here: I stand in awe of him.

John Wooden,
former UCLA coach and a
member of the Basketball
Hall of Fame.

Credits:

Cover design by Phil Velikan

Inside flap photo by Tom Ponton

Introduction

Tom Bast, Director of Masters Press of Indianapolis, called in January 1997 and suggested I update my autobiography with another one because so much had happened in my life since *From Orphans to Champions* was published. While that book was still new in the stores, I received an offer of seven hundred thousand dollars to coach North Carolina State and two of my graduates, Sidney Lowe and Dereck Whittenburg. So that story is not in my first autobiography. That, and other events in the years since the book was published in 1979, prompted Tom to suggest I write a second autobiography.

I never really thought about a first autobiography, much

less a second. You don't go through your career thinking the world is clamoring to read the story of your life. And you certainly don't think they'll want to read it twice.

Still, when I thought about it, Tom's suggestion made sense. I have never had the opportunity to write the full story behind a dazzling offer from North Carolina State, and there were other stories that seemed worth telling — scholarships for our seniors, trips overseas, kids and former players in need of special help — one involving the kidnapping of Hillary Clinton's lawyer — visits to the White House at the invitation of Presidents Reagan and Bush after earlier visits with Presidents Kennedy and Ford, and so much more.

Besides, as the reader will see in Chapter One and from Chapter Eleven through the rest of the book, a second autobiography would give me a vehicle for urging people to sign up as future organ donors, after my near-death in 1996, when a liver transplant made possible by a heroic woman I never knew saved my life. As I've said throughout my career, the greatest reward I find in teaching and coaching is the opportunity to touch people's lives. Organ donors, however, do even more than that. They save people's lives. Another book might produce more organ donors — and save more lives.

That clinched it.

Morgan Wootten
Hyattsville, Maryland
July 1997

Prologue

I take my seat on the bench, looking around DeMatha High School's tiny gym as I do. The scene is the same as virtually every other game I've coached at DeMatha — The walls are covered with banners signifying city and national championships. Our nationally famous pep band is playing our school's fight song. The stands, silent and empty only an hour before, have come alive with an overflow crowd of our students, their families and our other supporters in the larger "DeMatha family."

Only one thing seems different. My assistant coaches are not next to me on the bench. I become confused when I realize the game has already started, and I hadn't even noticed it.

I put out of my mind, as I have every game this season, my awareness that the disease which has been systematically destroying my liver over the past ten years is worsening rapidly. Only my wife, my children and their spouses know that if I do not receive a new liver in the next eighteen months, I'll die.

I strain to see the game, to reorient myself, but I can't see the action clearly. The game is moving quickly. Everything is blurry, like a movie out of focus. I reach to straighten my necktie, but I feel my skin instead. I look down and see I am wearing a player's uniform.

Suddenly, I become excited. I know this is a big game. I can feel it, as I do before every big game — the shouting students, the pep band, the shrill referees' whistles — like every big game I've ever coached. But there's a difference. Somehow, at the age of sixty-five, I'm going to play in this game, the first time I've played since my days at Montgomery Junior College in Silver Spring, Maryland, forty-five years ago.

But our coach in this game is Saint Peter, looking exactly the way you see him portrayed in paintings and sketches — a thick white beard, a full head of white hair, wearing a flowing robe and carrying himself with an erect bearing that gives him even more of a commanding appearance.

He is standing next to our bench when he turns and calls down to me to come up to him. I run up, but then he holds his hand up, turns toward me and says, "Go on back. I don't need you right now." I go back to my place on the bench and sit down again.

Was that dream God's way of telling me He was not ready for me?

— A dream by Morgan Wootten while unconscious following a liver transplant in July, 1996.

Foreword

BY JAMES BROWN
FOX-TV HOST AND
ANCHOR

L earning under Morgan Wootten for four years, both in the classroom and on the basketball court, constantly reinforced everything my mother and father taught me at home.

I had the pleasure and the honor of playing for Morgan and being taught by him for four years at DeMatha High School, from 1966 to 1969. Those were tumultuous years in American society, with protests over the Vietnam war, riots following the shooting death of the Reverend Dr. Martin Luther King, Jr., and the long, hot summers of civil rights demonstrations and anti-demonstrations.

Through it all, Morgan not only helped to put matters into perspective, but remained as solid as an oak tree to all of his student-athletes, never wavering in his beliefs or his commitments. His message to all of us remained the same about what he always called "the proper order of priorities — God first, family second, education third and then basketball, or anything else, no higher than fourth."

All of us believed that message, and still do, because Morgan is that rare human being: one who practices what he preaches. We didn't just hear him say those things — we saw him apply them every day in the things he did and said. When he collapsed and almost died in July, 1996, he faced the ultimate test of his deep faith. When he survived and made his remarkable recovery, the rest of us saw the rewards of that faith.

One of the first times I saw Morgan practice what he preaches was when my mother brought down her wrath on him. I was supposed to be home from school no later than 6:30 every afternoon — no excuses. And it didn't make any difference whether I was playing basketball for DeMatha or the Chicago Bulls — 6:30, young man, in the kitchen, doing your homework.

When 6:30 came and went one day and I was still a no-show, my mother called school and asked to speak with

Morgan. She was told he was in the gym at basketball practice, but that didn't make any difference. She wanted to talk to him. And she did. Morgan came to the phone, and she reminded him what time it was, and that a high school boy's proper place at that time of the evening was home, and doing his homework.

Morgan offered no defense, agreed with her and hurried up the end of practice. Then he called me at home later and asked me to thank my mother for reminding him of the proper order of priorities. He never tried to alibi his way out of it. He just said she was right, and that he was grateful to her.

I remember, too, how loyal and supportive he was when I had to decide where to attend college. He and Dean Smith are extremely close friends, and Dean made it very clear how much he wanted me to come to North Carolina on a basketball scholarship. I wanted to go to Harvard instead and major in economics.

Morgan never pressured me to go to North Carolina and never told me that playing for Dean would enhance my chances of playing in the NBA. Instead, he gave me the best neutral advice he could and told me, "Here are some criteria you should consider." He also said, "James, basketball is only one factor in the equation. Look at life." He reminded me of one of his messages to all of his athletes: "Don't let basketball use you. You use basketball."

When I eventually told him I had decided to go to Harvard, he said, "I'm proud of the decision you made."

To say that Morgan Wootten has touched people's lives understates the case, because he has done so much more than merely touch lives. He has guided them, influenced them in the right direction and always been there for all of his students and athletes for advice or for help in getting over some of the bumps in the road.

I was honored to be one of Morgan's players and one of the students in his ninth grade world history class. Today I remain honored that, in so many ways and without even realizing it himself, Morgan is still my coach and my teacher.

A COACH FOR
ALL SEASONS

One
A MONTH OF MIRACLES

Morgan Wootten was dying — unconscious and lying in a pool of his own blood. In the post card setting of Maryland's Catoctin Mountains next door to Camp David, he had collapsed in a men's room doorway, the victim of primary biliary cirrhosis, a rare liver disease with no known cause.

To friends and fans, he always seemed to have it all — a wife and family any man would be proud of, a record and stature unmatched in his profession, and popularity among the general public that any politician would envy. But now, in a split second on a perfect July Sunday afternoon at Mount Saint Mary's College, he was suddenly fighting for his life.

Wootten is a high school basketball coach, the most successful *and respected of all time, at DeMatha High School in Hyattsville, Maryland, just across the state line from Washington, D.C. Now sixty-six, he has been teaching boys about sports, history and life since Harry Truman was president and Wootten was the 19-year-old coach of a baseball team at an orphanage that never won a game.*

His DeMatha teams have won 1,122 games and lost only 170 while winning five national championships. His won-lost percentage is the best by far at any level — high school, college or the NBA. As one writer put it, "His teams have averaged twenty-nine wins and four losses per year. Imagine going 27-6 one year and having to explain what happened."

Yet Wootten tells his legion of friends in the news media and others, "I never say to my players at the start of a season, 'We need to win so many games this year,' or, 'We need to win this or that championship.' My goals are related more to the opportunity to touch lives, to see the members of this year's team go on to be productive citizens and lead good lives, and for DeMatha to play an important role in their young lives as they develop into outstanding human beings."

Like his counterpart at the college level, John Wooden, the Hall of Fame coach who guided UCLA to national prominence, Wootten achieves winning seasons while not making winning the primary goal itself. "That's a stumbling block," he says. "It gets in your way. It's like someone who makes being happy his or her goal. You cannot concentrate on being happy. Happiness is one of the by-products of living a good life and working hard to achieve your goals. It's the same way in athletics or any other form of competition — winning and championships are by-products of larger, more significant goals and having the right values and attitudes."

In 1965, in his ninth season at DeMatha, Wootten's team handed Kareem Abdul-Jabbar, then Lew Alcindor, the only defeat of his high school career. Twelve of his players have made it to the NBA including Adrian Dantley and Danny Ferry. Eleven former players or assistants have become head coaches or assistants at the college level including head coaches Jack Bruen of Colgate, Tulane's Perry Clark, Marty Fletcher at the University of Denver, Mike Brey at Delaware, Stetson University's Murray Arnold and Ronnie Everhart of McNeese State.

Another former Wootten player, Sidney Lowe, became an NBA head coach with the Minnesota Timberwolves and is now an assistant coach of the Cleveland Cavaliers, Danny Ferry's team. Still another Wootten and DeMatha product, James Brown, who also played in the NBA, is one of America's best-known sportscasters on television.

In 1980, Wootten turned down an offer of seven hundred thousand dollars-plus from North Carolina State, a decision which reflects his average-guy lifestyle. He relies on his wife to pick out clothes that match for him. He never wears a suit to a game but favors sports jackets with shirt and tie instead. He drives a car that the rest of us can afford, too. A believer in Ben Franklin's advice about early-to-bed and early-to-rise, he questioned a friend when Johnny Carson was leaving The

Tonight Show after thirty years, "This Johnny Carson — does he have a TV show of some kind?"

Three years after Wootten's turn-down, N.C. State, behind the leadership of two of Wootten's stars, won the national college championship — the Final Four. Sports Illustrated once ran a big spread called: THE WIZARD OF WASHINGTON. People magazine called Wootten "a real sports phenom." Time said his achievements are "astonishing."

In a role like Bing Crosby as Father O'Malley in Going My Way or Spencer Tracy as Father Flanagan in Boys Town, the record Coach Wootten is proudest of is this: In one special period of thirty straight years, every one of his DeMatha seniors — one hundred and seventy-five students, from his biggest stars to the lowest substitute on the far end of the bench, even the manager in some years — won a full four-year scholarship to college. Since 1960, over 95 percent of DeMatha's basketball players have won full college scholarships.

He has been to the White House to meet Presidents Kennedy, Ford, Reagan and Bush. He has spoken to audiences in Greece, Italy, France, Belgium, England, Canada, Brazil, Australia and Taiwan as well as forty-six of the fifty states. In a hundred speeches, seminars and clinics every year, his audiences are coaches, teachers, college students, association executives and leaders of America's biggest corporations — AT&T, IBM, MCI, The Gap stores and General Motors.

In 1991, he was selected by the Walt Disney Company as its Sports Teacher of the Year for his remarkable success as a teacher of basketball and, more than that, a molder of outstanding young men. With all this success and acclaim, if you ask Morgan what part of his career means the most to him, his simple answer is, "The opportunity to touch people's lives."

All of this, including his very life, was rapidly slipping away from Wootten as he lay on the floor at Mount Saint Mary's. This is the story of what happened that afternoon, of the times when Morgan Wootten touched people's lives — sometimes without even knowing it — and when others touched his.

I collapsed at my summer basketball camp, while opening the door to the men's room. I fell through the doorway and into the men's room as the door closed behind me. Fortunately, two of my camp counselors, college basketball players, happened to be walking behind me. Seth Schaffer, who plays for Jack Bruen at Colgate, and Adam Heck of Ithaca caught a glimpse of me as I went down. They told Jack later, "Coach, another fifteen seconds and we never would have seen him."

If they hadn't, I would have remained on the floor inside, unconscious and unseen, in an empty and seldom-used men's room. I could have bled to death. Their presence in that hallway and the fact that they turned my way in the same split-second as I was falling was the first

Morgan Wootten with every coach's standard equipment — a ball and a whistle.

in what became a month of miracles.

My son, Joe, who is on my coaching staff, immediately told Seth to call 911 and get our camp trainer, Bert Lentz. They did what they could until the team of emergency medical technicians arrived in an ambulance.

Joe rode in the cab of the ambulance to Gettysburg Hospital. He tells me it was a harrowing ride of nine miles, which was made even scarier for them because my blood pressure was plunging. At one point, the crew had to pull off the road to reduce the vibration and noise and because their instruments were showing I had almost no blood pressure at all. Somehow my pressure began to come back. Miracle Number Two.

My wife, Kathy, a registered nurse (Miracle Number Three), drove up immediately from our home in Hyattsville and saw me in the emergency room, fighting for my life and spitting up blood. Two weeks later she told me the blood was "coming out of your mouth like a fountain."

Eventually the doctors at Gettysburg, talking by phone to their counterparts at Johns Hopkins University Hospital in Baltimore where I was on the list for a liver transplant, were able to stop my bleeding. Miracle Number Four.

I was immediately evacuated by helicopter to Hopkins, twenty minutes away. It was perfect flying weather — Miracle Number Five to anyone familiar with the violent thunderstorms that typify summer afternoons in that part of the country. At Hopkins, Dr. Paul Thuluvath took emergency actions to stop my blood from backing up and coming out through my mouth. He needed to keep me alive long enough to get a liver. He was successful — Miracle Number Six.

My job on July 7, even though I didn't know it because I was unconscious, was to stay alive long enough for the program to find a liver for me. It took three days, and the stories in the Washington and Baltimore newspapers that I have since read, and those on the evening news on TV, which I have seen on video tape, said I was running out of time — fast.

The dramatic news that my family was waiting for came Tuesday, when a liver arrived at Hopkins. I was still unconscious and had been for three days and would be for another week, but the staff prepped me for the surgery, which normally lasts eight hours. Kathy and the kids were ready too, but then their hearts sank. Word came that the liver was too fatty, unsuitable.

At 5 A.M. on Wednesday, my family received a second bulletin: Another liver had just arrived — a healthy one, from someone who had just lost her fight to save her life while I was fighting to save mine. Miracle Number Seven. I was in surgery at nine. Five and a half hours later, two and a half hours faster than normal, I was being wheeled out of surgery and into the intensive care unit. My doctors, headed by my surgeon, Dr. James Burdick, said the excellent condition of the liver and the way my body accepted it so easily was another miracle — Number Eight.

As far as the media and the public were concerned, my drama lasted one month and two days, from the time of my collapse until the day I went home from the hospital. They didn't know that this drama unfolded over a stretch of twenty-five years, dating back to 1971, when I began getting an annual physical because I had turned forty.

I passed that first one with flying colors, except my liver levels were elevated, indicating an infection or irritation. It was a concern, but not a crisis. I didn't tell anyone except Kathy. The doctors tried everything — a special diet, no alcohol — nothing made a difference. Five years before my collapse at Mount Saint Mary's, the liver showed signs of more irritation. A specialist, Dr. Donald O'Kieffe, spotted the reason — PBC, primary biliary cirrhosis. Suddenly, what had been a concern became a crisis.

Dr. O'Kieffe said, "The bottom line is we don't know what causes it. What we do know is that the immune system turns on you and decides to attack the liver as if it's a foreign object." He said if I lived long enough, that's what would happen, and I would need a transplant. What may have started when I came down with hepatitis during an outbreak of that disease forty years earlier at Saint Joseph's Orphanage, where I began my coaching career, was now threatening my life.

As Kathy and I worked our way through those five years, we went into our own denials. I tried to deny to myself that things were really that bad. I told myself my fatigue was just age, that this must be what it feels like when you enter your sixties. Kathy says she told herself the same kind of things. But while we were in our separate denials, both of us were doing plenty of serious praying.

Then came my collapse — and my recovery, thanks to someone I never met, someone who donated her liver that someone else might live. I went home one month and two days after my collapse. Three months later, when our team held its first practice for the new basketball season, I was there, reaching one of two goals I had set for myself at the hospital. Eight days after that when our son, Brendan, was married on Long Island, I was there, too, reaching my second goal.

Even in illness and convalescence, you can touch people's lives, sometimes without knowing it. Something that happened while I was recovering at home from my transplant proves it.

Thirty miles up Interstate 270 in Frederick, Maryland, only a few miles from where I collapsed in July, a 16-year-old high school student was filling out his application for a driver's license. The *Baltimore Sun* reported that his father, Tom Dickman, a high school coach himself at Frederick's Thomas Johnson High School, noticed that his son, Chad, had checked "No" where the form asked if he wanted to be an organ donor in case he was killed in an accident.

The paper quoted Coach Dickman as saying, "I don't want to tell you what to do, but remember Coach Wootten just had a liver transplant. If it weren't for that, he might not still be around."

Chad filled out another form. This time he checked "Yes."

Then there are those whose lives you touch directly, young men you've worked with to steer them in the right direction, many times to a college education they might never have received, sometimes away from a life of crime, sometimes to make them believe in themselves when others didn't, other times to help them overcome a tragedy in their young lives — and always, always remembering Winston Churchill's brief but telling advice to other young men in wartime England in 1941: "Never give in..."

◆ ◆ ◆

I never had any intention of becoming a coach. I wanted to be a lawyer. I was on a debating team in the ninth grade, and we never lost a match. We won all nine of our debates, and from that early time I began to think I might be cut out to be a lawyer and maybe even run for office. But then fate, or the Good Lord Himself dressed up in a nun's habit and named Sister Batilde, stepped in and steered me in a different direction before I knew what hit me.

It happened in March, 1951, when the Korean War was still in its first year. I was still only nineteen years old and a coaching career was the last thing on my mind. Like every other boy my age, I was sweating out whether I might be drafted and sent into battle. My good friend, Tommy Clark, was vulnerable too, but on this day we were headed to Saint Joseph's Home for Boys on Bunker Hill Road in northeast Washington. Tommy was to be interviewed for the job of baseball coach by Sister Batilde of the Order of the Holy Cross. She was the Mother Superior of the orphanage. I remember pulling up a winding driveway to a big red brick building on top of a hill. Around the building were open fields and a swimming pool that was showing its age.

As we climbed out of my ten-year-old 1941 Buick with more than a hundred thousand miles on it, I remember thinking to myself, "So this is what an orphanage looks like."

About halfway through the interview, Tommy, who had been talking me up earlier, nods toward me and says, "Hey, Sister — he's a candidate, too." By then he wasn't kidding me. I knew what he was doing. He was losing interest and was pushing me as his way of getting himself off the hook.

So Sister Batilde turned toward me and said, "He

Bruce Reedy Photography
Coach Wootten communicates with the officials.

certainly sounds like the man for the job." Then she set forth the terms of the deal: Seventy-five dollars a month. No, not a week. A month. Practice every day including weekends. And supervise evening study hall for the seventh and eighth graders every night.

Then she smiled angelically at me and, without giving me a chance to open my mouth, said, "See you Monday."

To this day I don't remember ever accepting the job.

There I was, a real coach — not just some volunteer but a professional who was actually getting paid to coach. There was one complication — at least: I had zero qualifications. No coaching experience of any kind and coaching the one sport I knew nothing about and working with kids only five or six years younger than I was, kids who were old enough to be my brothers.

That didn't sound like any formula for success to me. It turns out it wasn't, at least not right away. That baseball team played sixteen games, and we never won one. As if being 0-and-16 for the season isn't humiliating enough, we were never in even one game. Every loss was a blow-out. We lost games by twenty or thirty runs. They were called after three or four innings because of the league rule limiting games to two and a half hours.

We were a sorry-looking team, too. You could tell we were a team of orphans. The other teams had first-class uniforms, with the team's name on the front and the player's number on the back. Our players were dressed in plain white T-shirts and blue jeans — then called overalls.

Winston Churchill would have been proud of those kids — they never gave in. I told them the same thing after every loss, the same message I still give to my teams almost a half-century later: "Show me a lot of class. No moaning, no groaning. No arguing with teammates or anyone else. No complaints about the weather or the umpire or injuries."

Then I always told them one of the central messages of athletics and life itself: "If we're not good enough now, we'll have to work harder to get better."

When the season was over, they asked me to come back in the fall and coach them in football. They said they were better at that. It was an offer I couldn't refuse. I was learning more from those kids about some important things than they were learning from me about baseball.

Sister Batilde was loyal to me too, although after that first baseball game, I wouldn't have taken any bets on my job security. We dragged our weary bones back to the orphanage after getting clobbered by Saint Anthony's, 32-0. When we got there, our spirits felt a lift when we saw that Sister Malathon, who ran the kitchen, had put out some soft drinks for us in the cafeteria. It was a thoughtful gesture on her part. And when you're a kid, there's nothing like a nice, cold drink after a game to help you celebrate a win or survive a loss.

We were sitting there enjoying our drinks when Sister Batilde walked into our happy scene. Her face broke out into a bright smile as she looked at me and said, "You won, Coach?"

I said, "No, Sister. We lost." I didn't have the courage to tell her the score.

She didn't need any more information, just whether we won. She ordered those kids to get right up and march out of that kitchen and put those drinks back in the refrigerator. Nobody asked any questions. Sister Batilde was from the bottom-line school of athletics — either you won or you lost. And even if the team that beat us was the New York Yankees, that didn't make one bit of difference.

To say that things were better in the fall would be a vast understatement. By the time our baseball season ended, the boys and I had formed a real closeness. We were ready to take on the world. So what if we went 0-and-16 in baseball? We were going to get better and have a great time while we were doing it, and 0-and-16 didn't mean a thing to us. Just numbers — numbers we were going to change.

Our affection for each other, coupled with their ability and experience in football, was a winning combination. Our football team won the championship of the Catholic Youth Organization. The kids got to play their championship game at Griffith Stadium, where the Redskins and the Washington Senators played all their home games.

After that first year of baseball and then football, I became hooked on coaching because I became hooked on kids. At that orphanage, then as a junior varsity coach two years later at Saint John's College High School under my long-time friend, Coach Joe Gallagher, and at DeMatha High School, where I have coached for the last forty-one years, I was always surrounded by high school student-athletes — in the classroom as a teacher of world history and on the basketball court.

At the beginning of my second year at Saint Joseph's, I used some connections to get the new heavyweight champion of the world, Rocky Marciano, who had just defeated Jersey Joe Walcott for the title, to visit our orphanage. Pete Haley, Sr., the founder of CYO sports in Washington, talked him into driving out to Saint Joseph's after making a public appearance in downtown Washington.

The champ walked into the orphanage just as we were finishing our evening rosary. He talked to the boys in our auditorium and told them about his boxing career, his personal values and the importance of leading the right kind of life. He made the added point of encouraging them to get a good start in life even though their road would be harder at first than it would be for other kids. Then he opened the floor to questions. When he did, something happened that contained a strong message for me.

I was the only adult male figure in the lives of most of

the boys in that auditorium, and one of them stood up and asked, "Rocky, do you think you could beat Morgan?"

Marciano managed to keep a straight face and did a classy thing. He looked me over as if to size me up and proceeded to give a serious answer to what he knew was meant as a serious question. He shook his head and said, "I don't really know. It would be a great fight. I'm a little bigger, but it would be a terrific fight, no question about it."

The kid said, "Nah — I don't think so. I think Morgan would kill you."

The room broke up in laughter, including my own, but that incident told me two things: I was reaching those boys, and I was meant to be a coach.

Two

After two years at Saint Joseph's and two more under Joe Gallagher coaching his jayvee teams in both football and basketball at Saint John's, a military high school across town, DeMatha called. And I turned them down.

The school's principal, Father Louis, offered me the job of basketball coach, but I was just getting adjusted to a full load, coaching two of Joe's teams and teaching history full-time. I told Father Louis I didn't think I was ready to become a head coach at the varsity level.

The next year, Father Louis called again. This time I knew I was ready. In the fall of 1956, when President Eisenhower was campaigning against Adlai Stevenson for the second

19

time, my relationship with DeMatha began, when I was twenty-five years old and DeMatha was only ten years old itself. That was forty-one years ago, and today, eight presidents after Ike, the relationship endures.

It's a Catholic boys' school named in honor of Saint John DeMatha, a young French priest who established the Trinitarian order of priests and brothers eight hundred years ago. As their mascot, the students and faculty chose the stag, an animal found in the forest of Cerfoid in France, where John DeMatha spent many hours in private prayer and meditation.

The school is a red two-story building with two long wings joined at a right angle, supplemented in recent years by a four-million dollar wing and a new student center, in a quiet setting one block from busy, commercialized U.S. Route One in Hyattsville. A monastery sits only a few feet away and serves as living quarters for the priests and brothers of the Immaculate Heart of Mary Province of the Order of the Most Holy Trinity, the men who teach at DeMatha and operate the school.

Today DeMatha has an enrollment of nine hundred and forty students, all boys, who come to school in coat and tie, study the classics but also use state-of-the-art computers and other learning equipment and receive a solid all-around education to prepare them for college and adulthood. They also get to root for championship teams in a variety of sports, not just our basketball teams.

I went to DeMatha at a salary of thirty-eight hundred dollars a year. For that amount, I was the head football coach, head basketball coach, assistant baseball coach, athletic director, world history teacher five periods a day five days a week, and the one who called the numbers at Bingo every Tuesday night.

At the start of my second year, they said they wanted me to work full-time.

◆ ◆ ◆

In my first twenty-five years there, our basketball teams won ninety percent of their games while playing the toughest high school schedule in the country. Both the percentage and the toughness of the schedule are the same today. To be the best, you have to beat the best. And you can't do that if you don't play them. It's not unusual for our basketball schedule to include four or five state champions.

Atheneum Publishers released my autobiography, *From Orphans to Champions*, in 1979. In it, we told the story of my first thirty years as a teacher-coach, about those special days at the orphanage, about learning so much from Joe Gallagher at Saint John's, winning championships at DeMatha, handing Kareem Abdul-Jabbar his only defeat at Power Memorial High School in New York, our undefeated season in 1977-78 after touring Brazil the previous summer against the best high school teams there, helping kids win scholarships to college, and helping other kids, for whom college was the least of their worries.

We wrote about the orphans at Saint Joseph's. One started stealing. The police brought him back to the orphanage several times after they caught him trying to steal. I pulled him aside one day and laid it out to him: "I hope you become the best athlete you can and later the best citizen you can — instead of doing what you are now: trying to be the best thief you can."

The words found their target. I started spending personal time with the boy, even though I was still only twenty years old myself. I took him to my house so he could enjoy some of Mom's home cooking and had him spend weekends with us, in an environment where there were parents and brothers and sisters and a real bedroom instead of a dorm.

Today he's still in Washington, enjoying a successful professional career and well known to many people who will read this, all of whom would be proud to call him their own son. He was headed for a life of crime until someone gave him the greatest gift that adults, not just parents, can give children — their time.

Another boy at Saint Joseph's wasn't there because he was an orphan, or because he was a bad kid. His mother simply couldn't afford to keep him after his father deserted them. It broke her heart to give him up, but there simply wasn't any other way.

When he reached high school age, the nuns judged him to be incapable of meeting the academic requirements of a standard high school, so they were going to send him to a vocational training school to learn a trade. I wouldn't disagree with that in most cases, but this was different. I thought this boy had more potential than that, so I recruited a successful businessman and friend of mine, Johnny Ryall, and we worked out a plan.

The boy could live at my apartment, and Johnny would pay his tuition to Saint John's. We got him released from the orphanage and he came to live with me for two years. We spent many evenings and weekends at the Wootten home on Thornhill Road in Silver Spring. Then this story developed a happy ending.

His mother married again and could afford to keep him, so he went home — to his home — and to his new dad, finished his education and is a Washington success story today as a sales executive. Not just a salesman. A sales executive. In the years that followed, I have been best man at his wedding, Godfather to his son and his playing partner during many rounds of golf. He's made it big, just as Johnny Ryall and I knew he would, because someone gave him a chance.

And we made sure to tell the story about that game against Kareem, on January 31, 1965, when we beat Power

Memorial before a packed house of 12,500 fans at Maryland University's Cole Field House — before it was expanded to 14,500 seats.

We devoted three full chapters to that game in my first autobiography — preparing for Power, the game itself and avoiding a letdown after scoring such a smashing upset — so we won't write another three chapters here. Some of it, however, is worth repeating because it illustrates the value of being willing to make changes. It also shows again, in a different way, that Churchill was right about never giving in.

Kareem was seven feet, two inches tall even then, and Power had never lost a game in his time there. They beat us the year before, in the last minute, by three points, and Kareem scored thirty-eight points. Our strategy in the 1964 game was to let Kareem score whatever he could while we stopped everybody else.

For the '65 re-match, I reversed our strategy: We would try to stop Kareem. The other Power players would have to pick up the slack — if they could. If they couldn't, we would win.

After that close call against us the year before, Power was laying it all on the line again — a winning streak of seventy-one games against our own streak of twenty-nine wins. It was the high school game of the year in the entire nation, maybe of all time.

Photo by Fr. Ed Wagner

*DeMatha Principal John Moylan (left) and Morgan
Wootten look over Moylan's 1965 tennis racket, a key
instrument in DeMatha's victory over Kareem Abdul–
Jabbar's Power Memorial team in what many still
consider the greatest high school basketball game
ever played.*

On the day of the game — with the war in Vietnam getting hot fast and the eleven-day-old administration of Lyndon Johnson and Hubert Humphrey still making plenty of news, the only story on the front page of the *Washington Daily News* was headlined:

NATION'S FINEST
12,000 to See New York's Power Memorial and DeMatha
High Tonight

Right below that headline were two rows of pictures of the stars — Power's five starting players and its coach, Jack Donohue, and our five starters and me. Below that was a profile of each player — his full name, uniform number, height, weight, year in school and position.

Across the bottom of the page was another bold line telling readers of all the coverage inside:

See Preview Story, Cartoon, Complete Rosters &
Kiernan's Corner on Page 17

All this for a high school basketball game.

On the day of the game, two-dollar tickets were being scalped for twenty-five. Every Washington newspaper — we had three then — was there, and so were all the radio and television stations. The Baltimore papers and stations covered the game, too. The national news media also showed up — *Time, Newsweek*, CBS and NBC. People said at the time it was the greatest high school basketball game ever played. Many still say it.

I was confronted by a serious dilemma in preparing our team for that game: How does a high school team stop an opposing player who is seven feet fall? Thirty years ago, high school teams didn't have seven-footers. Maybe six-six, or six-eight or six-nine. But seven feet? Unheard of.

The solution came in a stroke of genius from my long-time DeMatha colleague and friend, John Moylan, who came to DeMatha when I did and is now our school's principal. I thought we had a decent chance of holding Alcindor's points and rebounds down to a reasonable level, but I was more concerned that he was going to hold our own point total down because of his ability to block shots all night long.

I told John I was looking for some kind of a team drill or technique to work on in practice that would help us to get our shots off over his seven-foot frame and his raised arms. I even suggested stationing one of our starters, Sid Catlett, under the basket on a ladder in practice and have our players shoot over him until they became accustomed to arching their shots much higher than normal.

John trumped my idea with one that was much better. He said, "Why not use my tennis racket?"

Brilliant! With a tennis racket, Sid, a future Notre Dame star who was six feet eight inches tall himself, could move around instead of being stationary on a ladder.

That's exactly what we did. Sid had firm orders from

me to block every shot he could. With his height and that tennis racket added to it, he looked like the Washington Monument in a DeMatha uniform. With his jumping ability added to everything else, our shooters had to put enough arch on their shots to bring rain. By the day of the game, the only way Alcindor was going to block our shots was to play with a tennis racket, too.

As our team prepared to take the floor against Power that night, I said something I've said to only one or two other teams in my entire coaching career: "Fellas, everybody knows what DeMatha does in big games."

We beat Power Memorial in another cliff-hanger, another three-point game, 46-43. We did it by stopping Alcindor and taking away Power's inside game, holding him to sixteen points, fourteen below his average, and by being able to score over him, thanks to John Moylan and his tennis racket.

Three

No one was more astonished than I was when North Carolina State's head basketball coach, Norm Sloan, called me in February 1980 and told me he was leaving State to take the head coach's job at the University of Florida. Norm and I had known each other for years by that time.

He was more than just a winning coach — he was also a motivator — so we related to each other well. I heard him talk at the clinic I conduct for high school and college coaches, and he spoke at our DeMatha sports banquets. He also spent a lot of time recruiting DeMatha players for N.C. State, including Sidney Lowe and Dereck Whittenburg, Kenny Carr, Hawkeye Whitney and Benny

Bolton, a recruiting strategy followed by the man who took the job after I turned it down, Jim Valvano.

All in all, Norm and I saw a lot of each other and spoke on the phone often between personal visits. Norm, it turned out, wasn't calling just to tell me he was leaving State. Over the phone he said, "I've talked to Willis Casey (State's athletic director) and told him, 'There's only one guy for you to get. Get Morgan Wootten if you can. It's that simple.'"

It was highly flattering, and more. The opportunity to become a college coach, especially in a big-time program at a major college in one of the best athletic conferences in the country — the Atlantic Coast Conference — is something many high school coaches lie awake at night dreaming about.

It was an even better dream in my case. Maryland is only one state removed from North Carolina. I've been there more times than I can count for DeMatha games. I was even born there, in Durham. I followed the North Carolina teams closely because my own alma mater, the University of Maryland, is also in the ACC. Many of my players at DeMatha went on to outstanding careers with ACC teams. I knew every coach in the conference because, like Norm, they come to DeMatha every year to talk to me about my seniors. And Lowe and Whittenburg were playing for N.C. State at that time, in a program that was destined to win the Final Four championship only three seasons later.

Casey called me right after that and offered me the job. Now I was on the spot. I had a decision to make — and what a decision. Opportunities are nice, but sometimes they are bad for your peace of mind. To say I was perfectly happy at DeMatha would be a vast understatement. I had been there almost twenty-five years, had achieved a certain level of success for the school, our student-athletes and myself, was able to support Kathy and our kids, was appreciated by the other members of the DeMatha family and had given no thought at all to moving up to the college level. Still ...

That's where your peace of mind gets knocked out of balance. Here I was, about to turn fifty years old, perfectly happy with everything about my life and my family. DeMatha had achieved that rarity in sports — an undefeated season and the national high school championship, our fourth — only two seasons before. Then we had another outstanding season the next year with Lowe, Whittenburg and Percy White, all seniors and stars.

That team proved to be just as memorable as the team before. We were on track to break the all-time Washington area winning streak of fifty-games set by the Archbishop Carroll team that included Monk Malloy, now Father Malloy, the president of Notre Dame, but we suffered injuries to White and Whit and had our streak snapped. With at least two of that threesome in the lineup, we never lost a game that year.

One game still sticks in my mind, in the Pepsi-Cola tournament in Lake Charles, Louisiana. We were playing Wheatley High of Houston, the Number One team in Texas and the state champions fifteen times, including five of the previous nine years. We were not too shabby ourselves — riding the crest of a winning streak that had reached forty-one games.

The game went five overtime periods. By the intermission after the fourth overtime, I was fresh out of strategic brilliance and was down to one last motivational quote — you guessed it — Winston Churchill.

That's always been one of my favorite quotes, but as we headed for that fifth overtime in Louisiana, I was feeling more than just admiration toward Churchill and his formula for success. I was feeling gratitude, too, because if he hadn't said that, I would have had to think up something myself, and by that point I might have come up empty in the motivational department.

I've always been big on motivational quotes. I still use them, not only as a means of motivating my teams but to motivate myself, too. I use them to illustrate to my basketball players what some of the most respected people in history have said on the subject of how to achieve success and the need to "pay the price" if you want to get there. I quote Red Blaik, the winning football coach at West Point in the 1940s and '50s: "Don't criticize success — analyze it."

There's the Boys' Town slogan which emphasizes loyalty and dedication with a drawing of one kid carrying another on his back and saying, "He ain't heavy, Father — he's my brother." And one of my favorite anonymous warnings: "If you hoot with the owls at night, you cannot soar with the eagles at dawn." And from another anonymous philosopher and wise person: "Success is failure turned inside out."

Some say those quotes are corny, and reciting them to high school students is even cornier, but it's hard for me to consider Winston Churchill corny. So I quoted him as our exhausted athletes took the floor for that fifth overtime in Louisiana.

Sidney Lowe was nothing less than brilliant for that whole game. Against a pressing defense from start to finish by an all-seniors team, Sidney played every minute and, as the point guard, committed only one turnover. But we were undermanned. Whittenburg suffered a hairline fracture of the small toe on his left foot and had to come out of the game.

At that moment, a DeMatha tradition was born. Bobby Ferry, a sophomore and the son of the Bullets' general manager, Bob Ferry, replaced Whit. Playing the last quarter and a half of regulation time and every minute of the five overtimes, with pressure on every shot and every free throw, Bobby, in only his sixth varsity game, scored twenty-five points on 7-for-12 shooting from the floor and

Morgan with longtime friend, mentor and rival Joe Gallagher in 1991, before Gallagher's last game as coach of Saint John's College High School in Washington.

11-of-12 from the foul line. He converted both ends of a one-and-one free throw situation with only seconds left in the second overtime to tie the game, 92-92, and keep us alive for a third overtime. He was only fifteen years old, but he was one of the leaders in our victory in what we now know was a preview of his outstanding basketball career. A few years later, Bobby was followed to DeMatha by his brother, Danny.

We won the game in the fifth overtime, 98-94, when Sidney Lowe also converted both ends of a one-and-one situation, and we went on to win the tournament. If you're wondering how the score could be 92-92 after two overtimes and only 98-94 three periods later, it's because neither team scored a point in the third and fourth overtime periods. That's what kind of a tension-filled game it was.

Something that was both surprising and regrettable happened after that game. Wheatley's coach, who had coached the school to five championships in the previous ten years, told Donald Huff of *The Washington Post*, "We are the most consistent winning team in the country. This year we don't have a good team..."

He went on to say that "my All-America, six-foot-six Roosevelt McGruder, didn't play, in addition to several other starters" who were injured. He didn't mention how crippled we were without Percy White and Dereck Whittenburg and how much pressure we were under by having to play a fifteen-year-old sophomore.

Climbing Mountains

Then he made a statement that was so surprising that I laughed when reporters told me about and asked for my reaction. He said, "I thought DeMatha was a good team, but there are at least ten teams in Houston that could beat them."

That's what broke me up in laughter. I told the reporters, "If there are ten teams in Houston that could beat us, I sure don't want to play them. I know for sure Wheatley isn't one of them."

The coach had said somewhat the same thing to me, telling me he was missing some of his starters. Heck, so was I. So what? One of the most important lessons for a coach to teach his players is to develop the willingness and the ability to overcome adversity. If you want to be a success in athletics, or in life, you have to adjust to changing conditions. There will be many times when a coach doesn't have all of his starters, just as there will be many times when you are working under less than ideal conditions in an office.

I told the coach that after watching him win his previous game by fifty points — 116-66 over Sulphur High of Louisiana, if he has four better players than those on the floor for that game, they should be playing in college.

The reporters asked me if our win over Wheatley compared to our upset over Power Memorial with Kareem Abdul-Jabbar. I told them it ranked fourth, behind the Power win, our upset over McKinley Tech for the Knights of Columbus tournament championship when our star, James Brown, was hospitalized with exhaustion, and a come-from-behind victory over Long Island Lutheran in 1969. That was a game when we were trailing by twenty-three points with seven minutes to play and ended up freezing the ball in the last minute for an 85-82 win. At the risk of offending Wheatley's coach, I told the reporters this win, sweet as it was, ranked only fourth among our most exciting victories.

I say his remarks were surprising and regrettable because of all the emphasis that many coaches place on winning and losing with dignity and good manners. That was one of the first lessons I learned from Joe Gallagher at Saint John's, and it's one I pass on to our athletes every year, and not just those on our basketball team. As DeMatha's athletic director, I have always made certain that we hired coaches in every sport who share that feeling and instill that attitude in every DeMatha athlete. That's why I was so sorry to hear such a reaction from another coach after a big game. It was a classic opportunity to reach his kids by using that game as something to learn from.

We were enjoying another successful season the following year when Norm Sloan called, followed by Willis Casey, followed by a third call from — who else? — N.C. State's two freshman guards, Sidney and Whit. They told me, "Coach, you have to come down here. We'll win the Final Four by the time we're seniors, maybe before that."

I talked to Kathy and the kids about it. We discussed it at dinner several times. It was a difficult decision for Kathy and me, but the kids each knew what they wanted us to do. The older kids wanted to stay because they had their friends and they were settled in school. The younger ones saw the opportunity as an exciting new adventure.

We took a vote several times. During the first round of deliberations, Carol, who was then entering her teens, asked, "Does this mean I can give up my paper route?" And all of the kids wanted to know if we could have a swimming pool.

Joe even tried to rig the vote with an ineligible voter, our family mongrel, Kenickie, who was named after one of the characters in the Broadway musical, *Grease*. Whenever we were discussing the question, Joe would look down at Kenickie, who would then, like any dog, look up and wag his tail. Joe would say with great excitement, "Look! Kenickie's wagging his tail! That means he's voting yes, too!"

As I continued to seek advice while mulling the opportunity over, the phone at home rang one night and Cathy, then a teenager and opposed to the move, answered it. Willis Casey was calling to talk to me. When Cathy told him I wasn't home, Willis, who was anxious to track me down, asked, "Where is he?"

Cathy said, "He's at the same place where he'll be a year from now — at DeMatha High School."

To my utter amazement and for reasons which I'm still not sure I understand completely, this was becoming the biggest sports story in Washington and was taking on a life of its own. It was on the front page — not the front sports page but the front page itself. It was one of the top stories on the evening news. Columns were written advising me what to do. Friends whom I respected said I should climb other mountains, that I had accomplished everything I could at DeMatha and now it was time to climb higher.

This went on for three weeks as I continued the deepest soul-searching of my career. I've always been so happy at DeMatha. When offers came, I was always flattered, including those from three Atlantic Coast Conference teams and one NCAA champion, but there was only one time before the N.C. State opportunity that I thought seriously about leaving DeMatha for a college coaching position.

That was in March, 1969, when Maryland University hired Lefty Driesell after I had been at DeMatha for thirteen years. Lefty was the head coach at Davidson College in North Carolina and was Maryland's first choice, and I was its second. I told the school I would take the job if Lefty turned it down.

As fate would have it, the weekend that Lefty was to announce his decision turned out to be the same weekend when DeMatha achieved one of its greatest basketball triumphs in the annual Knights of Columbus tournament,

Morgan Wootten and Bob Hope were honored by the Touchdown Club of Washington in 1976. Sitting in the middle is Hall of Fame quarterback Sonny Jurgensen.

upsetting McKinley Tech of Washington without our star, James Brown. J.B. was suffering from exhaustion for reasons which I'll get into in Chapter Six, when we talk about being recruited by college scouts and coaches. We were expected to be so much weaker without James that Tech would win in a romp — at least, that's what the "experts" were saying.

But Mark Edwards wasn't buying any of that. Mark, who later graduated from Georgetown University and is now an actor and producer, spent the game outrebounding two taller Tech players. In the fourth quarter, we were winning by twenty-two points. We won going away. I was so awed by this superhuman effort by my players in behalf of their fallen teammate that I put my head in my hands late in the game and prayed silently, "Please, God — let Lefty take the job."

We were celebrating with a victory dinner at Ledo's, an Italian restaurant near Maryland University and DeMatha, one of my favorite spots, when I received a phone call. It was Mark Asher of *The Washington Post*.

"Morgan," he said, "Lefty's taking the Maryland job. He just announced it on his TV show at Davidson." My prayer had been answered.

The next day, Lefty was at DeMatha — trying to recruit James Brown for Maryland.

The N.C. State offer eleven years later, to the month, was

the only other offer I ever considered seriously. That includes the time when Driesell left Maryland following the death of Len Bias in 1986. Maryland's chancellor then, John Slaughter, hired a high school coach, Bob Wade from Dunbar High in Baltimore, to succeed Lefty.

Over the years since, people have assumed that I would have jumped at the Maryland job in 1986, but they're wrong. By that time, I had no interest in coaching at Maryland, even though it is my alma mater and close to home. People ask me if I turned Maryland down. The answer is no. I couldn't. I didn't have the chance. I never heard from Slaughter or anyone else with the authority to interview me, much less someone who could offer me the job.

I would not have taken the job anyhow and probably would even have declined the opportunity for an interview. I just was not interested at that stage in my career after thirty years of success at DeMatha. However, I was flattered to have received many calls and messages from Maryland alumni and officials strongly supporting me. Even though I did not make myself a candidate, I received widespread community support from people who thought I should be the Maryland coach.

One interesting and amusing story involved a phone call from a highly placed university source who told me, "Stay right there by the phone. I just left Dr. Slaughter, and when I mentioned you to him, he said, 'As a matter of fact, I'm on my way to my office to call him right now.'"

But he never did. Instead, Slaughter drove to Baltimore-Washington Airport for a news conference and announced he was hiring Wade. Shortly after that, Slaughter resigned to take a job in California.

The four winningest high school coaches of all time, from left: Bob Hughes of Fort Worth, Bill Kruger of Houston, Morgan Wootten and Ralph Tasker of Hobbs, New Mexico.

Four

The N.C. State offer was enough to tempt anyone. It was a real attention-grabber, especially after Willis Casey spelled out the terms: a compensation package exceeding seven hundred thousand dollars over five years, including base salary, my own summer camps, my own radio and television shows — all that plus a free college education for all five of our children. And they would guarantee the sale of our house.

The day after Willis gave me the terms, that figure of $700,000 was in big, bold headlines in *The Washington Post*, and then all over the Washington news media. I don't know where they got the story — it didn't come from me

— but the Post was right on the money, so to speak. It had a funny psychological effect on me. It was staggering enough to hear Willis mention the components of the package the night before, but when I saw that dollar sign and those six figures behind it in that bold headline the next morning, it almost knocked me right off my feet. Our daughter, Carol, had it figured out — a hundred thousand for each of the seven of us.

I deliberated more. Vic Bubas, a great friend of mine who coached Duke to two Final Four appearances and was instrumental in raising college basketball to its current level of popularity, was commissioner of the Sun Belt Conference at that time. With all of his success and knowledge and the tremendous respect everyone has for him, Vic was one of the first people I wanted to talk to, so I called him. He said, "Morgan, if you have to climb that mountain, if you really need to see the other side and you have a fire in your belly to do it, I understand that. Then you should go for it."

Then he added, "But, if it's not your burning desire, and if you are really happy right now and feel fulfilled at DeMatha and think you really could not accomplish anything more at the college level in touching people's lives, then you had better take a good, hard look before you decide to go."

As his closing argument, he said, "You really should not go unless you are obsessed with a passion for climbing that mountain."

The situation was similar to the time I was approached about running for the United States Senate. A prominent senator's staff members had conducted a name-recognition poll throughout Maryland and found that I was known well enough to be a credible candidate and could run a respectable race against the incumbent. The staff members approached me with the information. They said they were anxious for me to run, and so was their boss, the senator from another state. But they added a decisive stipulation: "We don't want to lead a reluctant warrior into the ring."

I politely turned down that very flattering opportunity, and I was leaning toward doing the same thing with the N.C. State offer. In each case, I would have enjoyed the new position, but there were elements involved that I would not have enjoyed. As a high school coach, I was enjoying everything about my profession and my job, including my work in the classroom as a world history teacher four periods a day, working with high school-age students, spending more time with my family than I would be able to if I were on the road recruiting, and controlling my own schedule. I knew several former high school coaches who had moved up to the college level only to find that they missed the classroom and these other "fringe benefits" of life at the high school level.

I once received a hand-written note from John Wooden

Photo by Mike Gielen, Sr.

Duke Coach Mike Krzyzewski (right) and Morgan Wootten visit during Morgan's annual coaches' clinic at DeMatha in 1991.

quoting an anonymous poet on the subject of the good that teachers can do:

> "No written word, no oral plea
> Can teach our youth what they should be;
> Nor all the books on all the shelves —
> It's what the teachers are themselves."

I didn't want to walk away from that. I knew I would miss it too much. But to be fair to everyone concerned, I looked at all the advantages of the N.C. State offer. Everything seemed appealing. But when I looked at it as coldly and objectively as you can with an offer of that magnitude, the fire that is supposed to be in your belly just was not there. The fire in my belly was for what I was already doing at DeMatha.

By that point in my career, I had been around college coaches for many years. I got a good look at the lives they lead. It wasn't that I saw anything in their lives that I didn't want — it was that I saw so many things in my own life that I wanted to keep.

I asked myself, "Why should I go to North Carolina State just to prove to other people that I can succeed at that level? And even if I win there, what would be next — the pros? Then what? Start a league on the moon to prove I can win there, too? At what point do you draw the line?" The only people I had to answer to were my family and myself, and they would be happier if they knew I was happy and doing what I wanted to do. And all of us knew how happy and fulfilled I felt at DeMatha.

On Friday afternoon of the third week of this saga, I was talking to my friend and colleague since 1956, Buck Offutt. Buck and I started at DeMatha together, and we're both still there. He has achieved national recognition not only as a teacher and athletic coach but also as America's foremost expert in preparing high school seniors for their S.A.T. tests. Corporate presidents — even university presidents — send their children to Buck to prepare for those college tests. Buck is simply the best there is.

Buck has been an English teacher for all of his career, plus serving as DeMatha's baseball coach and as my line coach in football during our early years together. I was his best man at his wedding and I am godfather to his son, Mark.

We got to talking about the North Carolina State offer. I was still leaning toward saying no thanks — but, on the other hand...

That's how it had been going for close to three weeks now. There were still many factors, and so many of them were of major significance. I said, "Buck, you know this offer is incredible. It's unbelievable."

Then Buck said something that cleared everything up for me in an instant. He said, "You know, Morgan, before they put that figure of $700,000 in the headlines, you were inclined not to take the job. But after they did, you started thinking strongly about taking it. Is it the money that's going to make your decision? You have to remove the money and look at everything else. I know you're not for sale."

Presto! Once I did that, I knew what I wanted to do. The decision was an easy one. What Buck said knocked me off the fence I had been sitting on.

I called Willis Casey at N.C. State the next morning and turned down his offer and thanked him not only for thinking of me but also for his professionalism and integrity in our discussions. He represented his school with genuine class and dignity, and I was indebted to him for that.

That afternoon I released an announcement of my decision to the news media. I didn't want to seem to be getting a big head about all this by taking word of my decision to the press, but I thought the media deserved to hear the news straight from me and not from anyone else. The reporters had all been professional with me, had quoted me accurately every step of the way and had made those three weeks a lot less hectic than they might have been.

I also wanted to use my statement as a vehicle for saying to all the newspaper readers and TV viewers who would see the story the same things I had always emphasized to my world history students and my basketball players — my message about priorities.

In my statement, I mentioned my order of priorities —

God first, then family, then education, with basketball no higher than the fourth most important thing in my life. I mentioned that the amount of money North Carolina State was offering me was both flattering and tempting, "but money has never been mentioned in my priorities."

I acknowledged the public encouragement for me to climb new mountains. That was a valid point, one which deserved a response, so I told the media my view on that subject: "Mountains are where you find them. Every time I help a student in my history class or a player on the basketball court, I feel I have climbed another mountain."

I never regretted my decision. DeMatha has since won another national championship, our fifth. Our program has continued to win national and even international recognition. I have taught at clinics all over the world. With our players, we have met presidents and other celebrities.

I have never looked back at my North Carolina State decision, even though others have. I have had people tell me, "I don't know how you turned it down. It was so tempting — how could anyone resist it?"

Instead, I rejoiced for Sidney and Whit when they made good on their prediction to me by winning the Final Four championship in their senior years at State — on the '82-'83 team, in that memorable game at Albuquerque when Whit hit Lorenzo Charles with a pass that Lorenzo slam-dunked in the last second of the title game. Whit has taken all kinds of ribbing since then that it wasn't a pass at all,

Morgan Wootten signals strategy to his DeMatha Stags.

just a missed shot from half-court that would have been an air ball but Charles made a superhuman play by grabbing it and dunking it. But Whit swears it was a pass, and I'm sticking with him.

As I watched that game in our recreation room, I knew, of course, that it could have been me instead of Jim Valvano dashing down the floor with my unbuttoned sports jacket flapping as I ran, looking frantically for somebody to hug in my ecstasy, the way Jimmy looked. And, as Sidney and Whit had told me, it might even have happened a year earlier. We might have won two Final Fours instead of just one — who knows?

But that was the right decision for me. I knew it then, and I know it now. It was also the right decision for Jimmy V. to take the job after I turned it down. And Sidney and Whit got their national championships. Over a period of time, it became a story with a happy ending, a win-win-win situation — for Sidney and Whit, for Jimmy V. and for me.

Jimmy was honored at a luncheon at the Washington Touchdown Club right after the Wolfpack won the title in 1983, and I was happy to be one of the speakers. There I was, the man who turned down the job three years earlier, speaking as I stood next to the man who took it and won the national college championship with it.

I paid him a couple of compliments at the start of my remarks, then paused, looked at him sitting next to the lectern where I was standing, and asked him, "By, the way, Jim, just how is that job — pretty good?"

Jimmy V. laughed louder than anyone else.

Both of Coach Wootten's sons played basketball under him. The team Joe Wootten (right) was a part of went undefeated his senior year.

Five

One of my most satisfying victories was also one of my strangest. That was in March 1981, when Bobby Ferry was a senior and we upset Dunbar, which was undefeated and ranked number one in the nation, for the city championship.

I had been extremely uncomfortable the week before with what turned out to be clogged sinuses. In addition to the discomfort, my equilibrium was off, so I had trouble keeping my balance. I told my doctor he had to get me healthy again, because we were playing for the city championship Sunday at Cole Field House and I had to be there. He said that was out of the question, and he told me why:

57

"You won't even be able to stand up."

We made arrangements with the telephone company to hook up a connection between the DeMatha bench and my house. My assistant coaches, Joe Mihalic and Joe Cantafio, ran the team from the bench on one end of the phone and did a magnificent job.

We were losing by ten points at halftime, and I took the opportunity to reveiw the first half with the coaches. I suggested, "Tell them don't try to catch up all at once. Tell them we'll just chip away in the second half and play our way back into the game."

Howard Garfinkel, the operator of one of the most re-spected basketball camps in America, the Five-Star camp in Pittsburgh, told me later, "That was the greatest act since the Clydesdale horses."

After that flattering, dazzling offer from North Carolina State in 1980 and our victory over Dunbar via telephone in '81, three of the most successful teams in my coaching career came along — DeMatha's teams of 1984, 1988 and 1991. All three had that ingredient found on all champi-onship teams in every sport: They didn't just have great starters — they also had outstanding "finishers."

You don't hear much about finishers. All the talk, plus the prestige, is about starters, about players being the best on their team and winning positions on the starting five in basketball, or the starting nine in baseball, or the starting eleven on offense or the starting defense in football. But coaches will tell you they are looking for finishers, the ones you can rely on to make that big basket just before the buzzer, or get that two-run single that drives in the tying and winning runs or make that game-winning touchdown or that game-saving interception.

That's what finishers do. They win for you. Every athlete can be proud to be a starter, and should be, but they can be even prouder to be finishers. Their parents should also be proud that they can look out on the court or the field and see that the coach thinks their son or daughter is good enough and important enough to be out there when the game is on the line.

Our '84, '88 and '91 Stags showed how great our finishers were by their performances in nail-biting games against some of America's greatest teams. When their high school years came to an end, these same student-athletes showed they were still great finishers by finishing the most important thing in their young lives, even more important than basketball — their educations. Almost every player on those three teams graduated from college. One of the few who didn't, Jerrod Mustaf, who won a scholarship to Maryland University, left college after two years to turn pro.

Two of those teams, '88 and '91, had something else on them — my two sons. Their presence gave me new challenges and new opportunities in my relationship with

Brendan and Joe that any mother or father who has coached a son or daughter in any sport at any level can relate to. The subject deserves special coverage, which we'll give it later in this chapter in describing those two seasons.

As we headed into the 1983-84 school year, DeMatha was already on a roll, and it didn't have anything to do with sports in general or basketball in particular. It had everything to do with item Number Three in our order of priorities — education — the priority that comes behind God and family, if you have your priorities in order.

Our school was one of sixty selected from across the country for "Blue Ribbon Awards" as exemplifying the best qualities in America's private schools. We were chosen from among the 358 schools which applied out of the six thousand private schools in the country. Those schools who went to the trouble of applying and were confident enough of their chances were required to fill out an application form 28 pages long in a contest sponsored by the Council for American Private Education. The competition was financed under a grant from the U.S. Department of Education.

Our principal, John Moylan, was as ecstatic as the rest of us. John has always been among the most enthusiastic supporters of our sports program, and his son, Pat, was a member of our basketball team that year, but John always knew the proper order of priorities. When a reporter for

The Washington Post, Elsa Walsh, interviewed him about this honor, John told her, "Most people hear DeMatha and what do they think about? — basketball. The people in the know have always recognized us as a really outstanding academic school. But the people who read the newspapers and sports pages think of us only because of our teams. Finally, the teachers who labor year in and year out are getting the recognition that our teams have gotten."

John made another good point when he told the reporter, "If a team wins a national championship, people always wonder if they can also have the academic program to support it." Then he said flatly, "Our academic program is superior to all our athletic programs. This is kind of the frosting on the cake."

Mike Cullen, one of DeMatha's French and Latin teachers, received a well-deserved mention from John. "He's our Mr. Chips," John told *The Post*. "You never see his name in the papers. But he's the kind of teacher you would like your kid to be working under."

Our '84 Stags lost only two games, to one of our conference rivals, Archbishop Carroll High School, and to Henry Clay of Kentucky during a long road trip.

Danny Ferry was one of the leaders of that team as our power forward, even though he was only a junior, but he wasn't our only important player. That team was loaded with "finishers." Our center was Carlton Valentine, who later enjoyed a successful college career at Michigan State. Drew Komlo, who played college ball — football — at Maryland and Catholic Universities, was our other forward. Our point guard was Quentin Jackson, who led N.C. State — yes, that N.C. State — to the Atlantic Coast Conference championship and then played for the Harlem Globetrotters. Our shooting guard was Juan Neal, who became a star at Niagara University.

For our twenty-fifth straight year, every senior won a full scholarship to college, raising the total to one hundred and fifteen DeMatha basketball players who had won college scholarships over that period. Joe Gallagher of Saint John's asks his high school players this food-for-thought question: "After they take that basketball out of your hands, what are you going to do for an encore?" For the past twenty-five years, these DeMatha seniors were making sure they would be prepared for that day.

That team had what Earl Weaver, the Hall of Fame manager of the Baltimore Orioles, called "deep depth." Two examples were Mike Gielen and Steve Trax. Mike was our backup point guard, but he was so good he became the starting point guard at Harvard University and was its team captain not once but twice.

Steve was another of those special cases every coach gets from time to time, who needs and deserves a special kind of treatment because of his unique situation on the team, not good enough to start on a talent-loaded team but good enough to be one of your most important players if you place him in the right role. I called Steve into my office one day, told him candidly that he was not good enough to be a starter on a team so rich in ability, but that he was good enough to be a big help to us. Then I told him I was going to make him a promise.

"You're going to be the most famous sixth man in America," I told him. "I want you to tell your family and your buddies and your girlfriend and everybody else that if they come out to our games they're going to see you play, and I'm not talking about `garbage time' at the end of a lopsided game. You'll be in every game before the end of the first quarter. I guarantee it. And I'll make you another promise: If the first quarter is about to end and I haven't put you in the game yet, you come down to me on the bench and remind me. I'll put you in right then."

Steve got to enjoy his senior year far more than he had expected. He played a lot of minutes, was in every game early, and was one of our heroes in two of our biggest victories that year. As a reserve forward, he sank six of nine outside jump shots against Saint Nicholas of Tolentine, a New York school, to help lead us to a 59-53 come-from-behind win.

He didn't forget my promise, and he made sure I didn't, either. Near the end of the first quarter in one of our games, he came up to me and asked me when I was going to put him in. He got his answer: I put him in right then.

Steve pulled off the same kind of heroics in our game against Dunbar for the Washington area championship. Then Steve went to college and became one of the greatest three-point shooters in the history of Old Dominion University.

Pat Moylan, one of our shooting guards, gave us firepower coming off the bench, then played college basketball at Bucknell. Another reserve forward, Steve Hood, played for Lefty Driesell at Maryland and James Madison Universities. Mike Graybill, a six-foot six-inch forward, went to Boston University on a basketball scholarship and became an offensive lineman in the National Football League.

With that much depth, we were able to hold great practices, so we were always well prepared for our next opponent. Every coach knows that teams play the way they practice. My assistant coach, Mike Brey, who is now the head coach at the University of Delaware, and I took great pleasure in planning our practices because we knew the team was so deep that we would practice well, then play another great game.

We opened the season against one of the toughest teams in the country, Dunbar of Baltimore, coached by one of the winningest high school coaches, Bob Wade. Dunbar was riding the peak of a 59-game winning streak. The game was played in a big-time atmosphere, before a sellout crowd at Georgetown University.

Photo by Edward Potskowski

*President Reagan receives a DeMatha warmup jacket
following the team's championship season in 1988.
Coach Wootten is on President Reagan's right, and
Morgan's son, Brendan, is between the President and
Mrs. Reagan.*

Dunbar was in another zone in the first half. Not a zone defense but a zone, period. Wade's team missed only five shots, but we were still well within striking distance when the half ended. In our dressing room at halftime, I told our team, "Fellas, you're playing great. Just keep it up." Our players came back out for the second half with their confidence level just as high as ever and continued to play well. The law of averages caught up with Dunbar and its shooting percentage returned to something closer to the level experienced by human beings. We won, 76-73.

That team kept topping itself, reaching one high point after another all season long. In December alone, we played six undefeated opponents, including Mater Dei of Los Angeles, a perennial national powerhouse. We beat them going away, 66-51. Carroll handed us our first defeat, 88-81, but we were able to avenge that loss fourteen games later by beating Carroll for our conference championship, 86-69. That game before a packed house at my high school alma mater, Montgomery Blair, in Silver Spring, qualified us for the city championship game. We took the obvious route to victory in that game, making seventy-five percent of our shots in the first half. Three times we defeated the team ranked Number One in the nation that week by *USA TODAY*.

With help from Steve Trax and his three-pointers, we beat the other Dunbar, the Washington one, for the city title, 61-50. With our conference and city championships already to our credit, we made our annual trip to the Alhambra Catholic Invitational Tournament in Cumberland. Then something unusual and exciting happened, something today's young people would call "cool" (an expression, by the way, which we used ourselves in high school in the 1940s). We found ourselves playing the Canadian champions, Cathedral Boys High of Hamilton, Ontario, in the tournament finals and matching our seventeen-game winning streak against Cathedral's thirty-seven straight wins. It was billed as the North American championship game. We won by twenty points, 70-50.

After playing the hardest schedule in the nation and winning everything from our conference title to the championship of all of North America, *USA TODAY* declared us national champions for the fifth time and flattered me by selecting me as its Coach of the Year.

The Washington Post, one of the most prominent newspapers in the world, devoted an editorial to our season and the success of other Washington area teams that season. Right there in the same columns usually reserved for *The Post's* views on issues of war and peace, they ran an editorial headed, HOOP HEAVEN.

The Post said, "The best of basketball being seen anywhere these days is right here in Washington's high schools and universities." The paper praised the area's top high school teams plus Maryland, Georgetown and other universities in the region and said if you add all these great teams together, "you have — here goes —

Greater Washington, Basketball Capital of the World."

The Post was kind enough to mention our program because of our "old-fashioned philosophy" at DeMatha "that young men are there to do more than play games."

The editorial concluded with a compliment for all of us:

> "Even for the high schools and universities, the basketball season is long and the demands of playing heavy. That is why those players of all ages from all around the region who have managed to blend good basketball with scholastic achievement deserve praise for an impressive season."

That special school year was made even sweeter by the performance or our other teams in basketball and other sports. DeMatha won fifteen conference and tournament championships. We fielded twenty-two teams in twelve sports, and here is the most important and most rewarding statistic of all: 420 students, almost half of our enrollment, experienced the fun of playing high school sports that year.

When our players reported for our first day of practice — always November 8 — to prepare for our 1987-88 season, I had the same level of talent and depth as that '84 team, and I had something else — our older son, Brendan.

In that situation, I remembered the story that Al McGuire and Joe Gallagher tell. Al led Marquette to the national championship in the 1970s, before becoming a well-known basketball analyst on network television. Al had coached his son, Allie, at Marquette. So when Joe was about to coach his own son, Jay, at St. John's High School in Washington, he wanted to know if Al had any special advice that might help him in dealing with the situation.

Al told him about something that happened when Allie was a senior and good enough to crack the starting lineup. Al had the intelligence and the courage to play him as a starter, knowing that he might hear some talk that he was playing favorites. Early in the season, he got a visit in his office from one of his substitutes. Sure enough, the kid thought he should be starting ahead of the coach's son.

"I'm better than Allie," he told Al. "I think I should be starting instead of him."

Al calmly said, "Son, let me tell you two things: Number one — You're not better than Allie. You may be as good, but you're not better. And Number two — I like you. But I love Allie."

You don't have to be a professional coach to go through the unique experience of coaching your own son or daughter. Every Little League father or mother who has volunteered to donate his or her time to coach any sport can identify with Al in that story.

In my case, Brendan made it easy for me. With great maturity, he was able to keep things separate. At DeMatha, he called me "Coach." At home he called me "Dad." In the gym we never talked about home. At home, we never talked about DeMatha basketball, unless Brendan brought it up.

Our 87-88 team won thirty of its thirty-three games. We were conference champions for the twenty-fifth time and also won our tenth city title and our twelfth Alhambra tournament. And Brendan got to be a hero.

In our fifth game of the year, we upset Archbishop Molloy of New York, which had been the nation's top-ranked team in *USA TODAY's* pre-season selections, 68-66. Rod Balanis made two clutch free throws with fifteen seconds left. Patrick Henry High School of Roanoke, Virginia, beat us in our seventeenth game for our third loss. It was also our last. We won all of our remaining sixteen games, by an average margin of twenty points.

Brendan's moment in the spotlight — and in the pressure cooker — came in our city title game against Washington's public high school champions, Coolidge. With only twenty-four seconds left — while I'm sitting on the bench thinking to myself, "My goodness, what have I gotten him into?" — Brendan calmly sank two free throws to give us the lead. We won the game and the championship, 57-54, at Maryland University's Cole Field House.

For me, the way we won that game was almost spooky. I had a dream a few nights earlier that stuck with me, even though I usually can't remember my dreams. In this one, I dreamed that Brendan was at the foul line in a one-and-one opportunity to win the city championship. But I never found out what happened. But in real life, Brendan showed me.

I told Donald Huff of *The Washington Post* after the game, "He earned his keep for another week."

Brendan was very calm about the whole thing. He told Huff, "We work on situations all the time. We say the score is tied in the championship game, and you can win it with two free throws. I was pretty confident when I went up there."

That comment made me feel good, and not just because it was my son. It reinforced the value of good practices. Brendan was saying that preparing for that kind of situation by practicing under simulated conditions helped him to perform when he had to. Maury Wills, the base-stealing champion of the Los Angeles Dodgers in the 1960s, will tell you that it's wrong to say practice makes perfect. Maury says, "Perfect practice makes perfect." We try to come as close as we can to holding perfect practices and prepare our athletes for precisely the kind of situation that Brendan faced — and handled successfully.

Brendan told Charlie Hartley of the *Catholic Standard* later, "I've always wanted to go to DeMatha and to play basketball for them. I went out for the freshman team. At first I wasn't a starter, but I gradually worked my way

Bruce Reedy Photography

The coach reviews the team statistics with his team.
At his right is Danny Ferry, now a star with the
Cleveland Cavaliers in the NBA.

into the starting lineup. That got me going."

I never pressured him into attending DeMatha. I told him to go wherever he wanted to, as long as it was a Catholic school. He chose DeMatha, even though his role of being my son might be more of a burden than ever. He admitted to Hartley, "All my life, I've been Morgan Wootten's son, not Brendan Wootten. It's been frustrating at times." He wasn't alone. Cathy, our oldest daughter, had told me the same kind of thing a few years earlier. They never let that kind of talk or attitude bother them. All of us have always agreed with one of John Wooden's favorite quotes: "Those that matter do not mind; those that mind do not matter."

I always tried to apply my advice for other coaches to myself in coaching Brendan and Joe. I tell them that you should treat them the way they would want their own son or daughter to be treated. But you have to be careful not to go too far the other way. It's a delicate balance.

Still, the father-son situation gave me an opportunity to relate to the other players and to their parents, too. I told Brendan's teammates I knew from my own experience that their parents probably tell them they aren't playing enough. "Well," I told our team, "I get home and my wife, Kathy, tells me I'm not playing Brendan enough."

Coach Mike Krzyzewski of Duke gave Brendan some nice recognition. He sent me a note congratulating us on our city championship and adding, "It's amazing how much you can accomplish when your family helps you. I am really happy for you, but I am even more happy for Brendan!"

Our varsity basketball Stags were doing what other DeMatha teams were doing that year. Our school won eight conference championships including varsity teams in five sports — basketball, baseball, wrestling, lacrosse and soccer.

The news for our basketball opponents didn't get any better. Our junior varsity and freshman basketball teams also won their conference championships, the jayvee with a 20-1 record and the freshmen going undefeated over a nineteen-game schedule. It all added up to sixty-nine wins and only four defeats.

Our varsity opponents might have been looking at those numbers in another way: The two "farm teams" for our varsity — the jayvee and freshmen teams — had a combined record that season of thirty-nine victories and only one loss.

Three years later, with our other son, Joe, playing for me, we enjoyed an undefeated season. Our nation won a big victory, too. Our 1990-91 season was played against the backdrop of our war against Iraq in the Persian Gulf. The war started and ended during our basketball season, lasting only from January 17 until President Bush announced our victory on February 28.

The varsity wasn't the only DeMatha basketball team to go undefeated that year. Our jayvee and freshman teams did, too. None of the three DeMatha basketball teams lost a game. The varsity Stags were 30-0, the junior varsity went 21-0, and the freshmen were 23-0, a combined season's total of seventy-four victories and no defeats.

People started calling our varsity "The Untouchables." We won our conference championship for the twenty-seventh time, the Gold Coast Classic in Los Angeles, the Prep Star Shootout in Fayetteville, North Carolina, and the city title. We climaxed a storybook season by defeating nationally ranked Roman Catholic High of Philadelphia, 64-61, for the Alhambra tournament championship. We were ranked first in the Washington area by *The Washington Post*, eighth in the nation by *USA TODAY* and fifth in the country by ESPN.

Any man or woman who has coached their son or daughter probably feels the same way I did about coaching Joe that year or Brendan before him. I never thought they should receive special treatment just because they were my sons, but I never thought they should be punished for it, either. The Ivy League schools follow that same philosophy in their attitude toward all athletes: We won't give you preferential treatment just because you are an athlete, but we won't discriminate against you because of it. The Ivy League's attitude is that in the classroom, everyone is a student; on the athletic field or court, everyone is an athlete.

In that connection, Bob Milloy gets my vote as coach of the year, and father of the year, too. Bob is a high school football coach in Maryland, in Montgomery County, the county next to Prince George's County, where I live and where DeMatha is located.

After winning six state football championships at Springbrook High School in Silver Spring, just across the Maryland state line from Washington, Bob changed jobs so he could coach his sons in football. Even though he had established himself at Springbrook as sort of the Joe Gibbs of high school football in Maryland, he moved to the football coach's job at Sherwood High School, farther out in the country, to coach his older son, also named Brendan, and his other son, Robbie.

They weren't even old enough to play at the time, but Bob was looking to the future. He knew they had a chance to become good enough to play high school football, and he wanted to be there as their coach when they did.

Like all great athletes and coaches, it didn't seem to make any difference where he was. He is a winner wherever he goes. At his new school, he already has won two more state championships, and his eight titles are the record for the state. Now he is also getting to coach his own sons.

Brendan Wootten's attitude on the subject of being the son of someone whose name is known to the public is typical of all of our children. We were talking about it not long ago and he said, "You always told us at home that we can take away something from the tough situations in life, and that's how you grow. And in world history class you told us that the Greeks taught their people that true wisdom comes through suffering.

"It's not that I suffered by being known as your son, but through whatever difficulty and adversity were put in my way because of it, I gained some valuable wisdom on how to deal with the real world, how to work with people, and how to take criticism for what it's worth — or, in some cases, for what it's not worth."

Brendan had obviously given some thought to the subject. He continued, "Having learned how to cope with things partly through being your son, I was able to deal with other trials in college and now in my career on Wall Street. I look back now and say thank God I was known as Morgan Wootten's son while I was growing up. If not, I would have missed out on those tests and what I gained from them. It makes me almost feel sorry for those who haven't encountered adversity yet."

Joe's moment in the sun for DeMatha came in our city championship game against Dunbar of Washington. We were losing by seventeen points at the half and by eleven at the start of the fourth quarter. Those are big deficits to make up, especially in high school ball, where the quarters are only eight minutes long. Joe teamed up with our other guard, Duane Simpkins, later of Maryland University, in our trapping defense. Together they forced six or seven turnovers.

Then, with only one minute to go and down by four points, Joe drove the right sideline with the ball. Seeing he was trapped by Dunbar's double-teaming defense, Joe was able to jump out of the trap and throw a cross-court "skip" pass to Ted Ellis. Ted sank a three-pointer to cut Dunbar's lead to one point.

As Dunbar was bringing the ball up-court in its next possession, Joe stole the ball. Vaughn Jones hit his signature turn-around jumper in the final seconds and we were city champions again, 72-71. It was a fitting climax to a banner year for Joe. While he was helping our basketball team to a successful season, he was also winning membership in the National Honor Society for his academic work, which Brendan had done before him. And at our annual athletic awards banquet, he was announced as the winner of the annual Unsung Hero Award for our basketball team. He was able to look back on a remarkable accomplishment. As a starter on our freshman and jayvee teams and in his senior year, when he was a starter on our varsity, Joe's teams never lost a game. A perfect record — three years as a starter, three undefeated seasons.

Whether you are coaching your own son or daughter or someone else's, you owe them a proper coaching and teaching attitude and a good example in everything you say and do. The reason can be found in one line by Edgar Guest, the poet, in his poem, The Crate: "...There is no unimportant man."

For me, the most important event at each of my summer camps is the orientation meeting with my staff. That's where I stress to those who will be coaching our many teams of kids from seven to eighteen years old that they are going to have the privilege — and that's exactly what it is — of working with everyone's most valuable resource, our young people.

I remind them that Lincoln told us that if we want to find out what someone is like, give them power. I tell the staff that they will have more power during that camp than they can imagine, because they are going to influence the kids under their supervision for better or for worse, for richer or for poorer.

I tell them candidly that their kids may not remember what the coaches tell them about the technical or tactical aspects of basketball, but they will never forget the coach himself. No one ever does. I point out to our coaches that no one forgets his coach and what they were like — whether you were nice to them, whether you made them feel better about themselves, whether you were trying to help them or just putting in time on the job, whether you made the child feel important.

I remind our staff that nothing great has ever been accomplished without enthusiasm. If you are enthusiastic in your dealings with kids, they are going to be enthusiastic. If you are wholesome and good, they will realize that this is the right way to conduct themselves. And I emphasize that all of us are teachers — whether we are teachers in school or in some other line of work. Because of this, what we say is important, but what we do is far more important.

I tell our coaches that they hold one of the keys to success while they are working with the kids at our camps because the same ingredients that produce success in basketball produce success in life. We place the strongest kind of emphasis on the message to our kids.

In turn, we tell the kids at our camps that they won't hear bad language from us, and we don't want to hear any from them. We tell the boys and girls that we won't embarrass them, and they should not embarrass us.

At DeMatha, I stress certain valuable fundamentals to the coaches of our freshman and junior varsity teams and my assistants on the varsity. I distribute a list of nine general thoughts that are essential building blocks in our basketball program and in all sports at DeMatha:

1. The importance of one-on-one contact with our student-athlete.
2. The need for harmony within our coaching staff.
3. The recognition that once a decision is made, we are totally unified in every respect.
4. The importance of finding extra time to tutor or

help a kid academically in any way, which is always one of the most important factors in helping our overall program.

5. The need to avoid putting our players in win-lose situations. We put them in win-win situations.

6. The importance of realizing that we are leaders. A leader does not push — he gets a banner and says, "Follow me."

7. The need to remember that a leader does not have his people work for him but with him.

8. Our immediate concern: to train our players for the game and tomorrow's world. They will always remember you.

9. Two deadly diseases of coaching: a fear of losing and a preoccupation with winning.

Our freshman and junior varsity coaches at DeMatha are also given a list of my objectives for their programs so they can provide the support that is essential for the continued, year-to-year development of our varsity team:

1. To develop the best players for future varsity competition.

2. To play players at positions they will be able to play at the varsity level.

3. To treat everyone fairly but not necessarily the same.

4. To settle on your top eight or nine players by

January and make certain they are the ones that need the playing time, remembering that it would be very unusual for more than eight or nine players to make the varsity.

5. To watch carefully in practices to see if someone else is really coming on.

I distribute a five-point statement of my own coaching philosophy, in my own words, to our coaches before the start of each season. In the corporate world, it would be considered a "mission statement." It can be applied to any sport, and to any other endeavor in life:

1. Provide a wholesome environment where young men can develop themselves spiritually, academically and athletically.
2. As coaches, we should be the kind we would want our own sons and daughters to play for.
3. We must never lose sight of the fact that basketball is a game and it should be fun. We should never put winning ahead of the development of the individual.
4. Since basketball is a great teaching situation, we must use this opportunity to teach the young men about the decisions they will be making in many areas that will have long-range effects on the quality of their lives.
5. The bottom line is: What kind of experience was DeMatha basketball for each individual?

Photo by Michael R. Hoyt, The Catholic Standard

Joe Wootten is hoisted into the air by teammate Eric Contee as the horn sounds in DeMatha's 72–71 victory over Dunbar in the 1991 Washington city championship game. Coach Morgan Wootten called the victory "the greatest comeback in DeMatha history."

I tell the coaches of our three basketball teams at DeMatha and at our summer camps, "Never underestimate the power you have, for good or bad, or the effects you can produce with that power. It doesn't take any talent to send a kid home with his head down because you made an unkind comment to him or made him feel by your treatment of him that he's not as good as the other kids in camp."

Instead, the real talent as a coach, whether in a summer camp or at the high school, is to provide love and dedication toward the young people entrusted to your care, by finding reasons to congratulate them individually, by giving them a pat on the back and, most of all, by keeping the fun in things for them.

How does a coach or teacher accomplish this? Simple, by following these principles, especially the one about being the kind of teacher or coach you would want your own children to have.

Those finishers on both Brendan's senior team and Joe's — including Brendan and Joe themselves and every substitute — all finished college except one. Not all of them became stars, and not all of the colleges have big-time athletic programs, but those young men earned college degrees from the University of Pennsylvania, Virginia, Maryland, Georgia Tech, North Carolina at Wilmington, Mount Saint Mary's, Salisbury State, Old Dominion, Manhattan and George Washington University.

They proved they are winners, because they are finishers. They finish what they start.

Six

For a star high school athlete, his or her senior year can be a dream come true. Just ask Adrian Dantley or Danny Ferry. Or it can be a nightmare that lands you in the hospital. Just ask James Brown.

J.B. was one of the most heavily recruited high school basketball stars in America when he was a senior at DeMatha in 1969, but in a summer camp before his senior year, his home address and phone number somehow leaked out — or were leaked out — and college recruiters picked the information up through their highly efficient grapevine. The result was predictable. James was over-recruited all season long. Without our knowing it, he was playing ball and studying under unrelenting pressure, with phone calls late at night and surprise visitors showing up at his door unannounced and all kinds of other interruptions to his privacy and his time.

The strain on him, which had never affected his performance on the court or in the classroom, reached a climax in the annual Washington Knights of Columbus tournament at Catholic University. In the first quarter of the semi-final game, J.B. took himself out of the game, raising his hand to signal that he was either too tired or hurt. He wasn't injured, and I didn't understand how any player could be that tired in the first quarter, especially someone who was in the peak physical condition that was always typical of James.

He headed straight for our bench, found his vacant chair and sat down. The next minute, I was distracted by a commotion on our bench, so I turned to see what the problem was. I looked and there was James — flat on the floor, out cold.

The trainers and emergency medical technicians worked on him immediately and revived him quickly. Then they carried him out on a stretcher and rushed him by ambulance to Providence Hospital. Diagnosis: Exhaustion.

Unknown to any of us at DeMatha, J.B. had simply been up too late on too many nights on the phone and receiving unexpected visitors, all of them college recruiters. They just would not leave this high school kid alone. That's what can happen if you accidentally allow your students' home addresses or phone numbers to leak out, or if you give them out. You have to establish a strict security program, based on one of the best-known slogans of World War II: "A slip of the lip can sink a ship." It can sink a high school kid's senior year, too, and maybe his college future.

The James Brown story has not one but two happy endings. Happy Ending Number One: We won that game, but the next day we were underdogs against McKinley Tech of Washington for the tournament championship. Things were expected to be ugly for us.

Tech had whipped us by fifteen points earlier in the season, and without James in the lineup, we weren't given a chance. People were afraid things might become humiliating for us. Friends of mine called me at home and begged off, saying they weren't coming to the game because they didn't want to see DeMatha get embarrassed. They told me they were sure I would understand. I understood all right. I understood that they were throwing in the towel before the game or the day even started. But we weren't. When the players on that team quoted Winston Churchill about not giving in, they really meant it.

The DeMatha Stags played one of the greatest games in the history of the school. Our players added a strong motivational touch before the game by leaving J.B.'s chair empty and draping his warmup jacket around it. Mark

Edwards filled in for James at our power forward position and spent the game out-jumping Tech's taller players. At the half, we were leading by twenty-one points. The crowd found it impossible to believe. A remark that I overheard at halftime told me the fans still expected us to be over-run by Tech in the second half.

As I was getting a drink of water at a fountain while our players rested in the dressing room, I heard a fan say, "The way I figure it, if we can cut DeMatha's lead to ten by the start of the fourth quarter, Tech can still win." It was not an unreasonable estimate of the situation, but it was obviously a staged comment, said for my benefit. I normally ignore the remarks of the fans, but I considered this one an insult because it was not just some innocent conversation between this fan and some friend of his.

I turned to them and said, "I've got news for you. This game is already history." And it was. We won in a romp. And as the KofC officials were awarding our players their individual trophies as tournament champions, here comes James down out of the crowd and onto the floor to accept his in person. He had sneaked out of the hospital and watched the entire game from the stands without any of us knowing he was there.

Happy Ending Number Two is that J.B. got to go to the college of his choice after all that pressure from all those recruiters. Even though his privacy had been violated and he had literally been driven to exhaustion, he still had time

Chuck Daly (left), the new coach of the Orlando Magic, was Detroit's coach and former DeMatha standout Adrian Dantley (center), was one of the Pistons' stars when they practiced at DeMatha and chatted with Morgan Wootten in 1988.

to apply one of my suggestions: Never make your final decision while you're visiting one of the schools on your list. The atmosphere can get pretty heady for a high school kid with all the flattery, the big-time surroundings and the appeal of campus life. All of these elements can combine to influence the high schooler and sometimes lead him to make a decision that he might not make at home in the calm and removed environment back there.

James had his choice of almost any college in the country because he excelled as much in the classroom as he did on the basketball court. One of the schools he visited was North Carolina. He was highly impressed by the university and by the Tar Heels' coach, Dean Smith, a man so rich in dignity and integrity. J.B. felt himself leaning strongly toward UNC, but he remembered the guideline about not committing yourself while you're visiting a school, so he told Dean, "Coach, I'm ninety-nine per cent sure I'll come here, but I'll call you after I get back home and let you know for sure."

Not long after James returned to Washington, I received a phone call at DeMatha from Senator Ted Kennedy of Massachusetts. He is a Harvard alumnus, and he invited J.B. and me to visit him in his Senate office. James wanted to visit Kennedy, so we went down to Capitol Hill and heard the senator tell the high school senior all the advantages that were waiting for him at Harvard.

James had always placed a proper value on his education, and eventually he chose Harvard, even though he knew North Carolina's reputation as an outstanding university, too. He was able to choose Harvard because he had not boxed himself in too soon by making his decision while on a campus visit to another school. He became part of a "DeMatha connection," a term which I am flattered to say is also applied to other schools. At Harvard, DeMatha graduates were members of the starting basketball team for sixteen straight years.

James earned his degree at Harvard, was a pre-season all-American selection twice, played in the NBA with the Atlanta Hawks and is now one of television's most popular sportscasters on Fox TV.

Adrian Dantley had a brilliant future as an All-American at Notre Dame and an All-Star in the NBA ahead of him when he almost fell victim to a coach's recruiting charms. The coach was Maryland University's Lefty Driesell.

Lefty has come in for a certain amount of criticism over the years, especially during the Len Bias tragedy in 1986, but I've always liked him. At Maryland, he emphasized to his players that they should be willing to accept the will of God in whatever happens. He encouraged them to "keep your head on straight." At the start of their freshman year, he made them write a composition to be handed in to him on what they want to achieve in college — in basketball and as a student and a person — because he believes strongly that to be successful you need goals.

Lefty wanted Dantley in the worst way, so he pulled out all the stops. Adrian was well known to college coaches and scouts as early as the ninth grade, so by his senior year at DeMatha the whole world knew about him and wanted him.

He and his mother, Virginia, followed my guidelines for dealing with recruiters, especially my fundamental rule: Let me be your buffer by telling anyone and everyone that they have to go through the coach. Adrian did that, was able to keep his sanity as a senior because his phone wasn't jumping off the hook, there were no surprise visitors showing up at home, and all the letters from recruiters were coming to DeMatha. He was able to enjoy his senior year of high school, something every senior is entitled to, and he reached a new level as the star of our team.

The first step in our set of guidelines to help our seniors and their families to control the recruiters and their pressures is simple: They should not give their home address or phone number to anyone. Period.

Step Two: They should direct all coaches, scouts, recruiters, alumni, news media and anyone else asking for such information to me.

Step Three: They must fill out a questionnaire which I have used over the years to state whether they want to limit their choices to a particular geographical area, whether they prefer a large school or a small one, whether they are looking for a school that is strong in a particular academic program and specify any other criteria they might have.

That questionnaire becomes my frame of reference. If a coach or a recruiter from a large university contacts me about one of my seniors and that senior has told me on his questionnaire that he wants to go to a small school, I tell the coach his school does not meet the boy's criteria, and I tell the coach why. It ends right there. The coach doesn't waste any time, and the student hasn't been bothered.

It adds up to a lot more phone calls and letters for me than I would have to deal with otherwise, but every coach owes it to his seniors to give them this protection and guidance. You don't tell the students where to go to college, but you help him to get through the maze of information confronting every high school senior, while also avoiding the overpowering pressure that proved too much even for someone as emotionally and physically strong as James Brown.

Every so often during the recruiting process, I sit down with each senior and present him with the phone messages and mail from recruiters whose schools meet the boy's criteria. We review and discuss all possibilities by ourselves, in a calm and private atmosphere, which I can control so the student-athlete can stay relaxed and start making preliminary decisions without anyone pressuring him.

There are new and emerging reasons for coaches and parents to meet their responsibilities in providing the proper protection and guidance for their children in handling the pressure from college recruiters. These new reasons come in the form of some — not all, and not even most — of the coaches running AAU teams in summer games.

The AAU — the Amateur Athletic Union — is an old and respected organization which sponsors teams of high school basketball players all over the country every summer. Most of the coaches are fine, upstanding individuals. But —

Some AAU coaches have now worked their way into the college recruiting business, serving as intermediaries who promise to deliver a certain player or players to a given school for who knows what in return. In recent years they have started the practice of calling parents and players, then calling college coaches and promising to deliver that kid. It happened to the mother of one of my own players in the summer of 1997.

They start their calls to parents the same way. In this case it was, "I was just talking to Morgan and..." Then the coach always goes on to give the parent the clear impression that he has my blessing to approach that parent, when the exact opposite is true. This DeMatha mother was alert enough to remember our guidelines, so she said, "That's really nice, but my son's plate is full. You check back with Morgan. I'm sure he'll give you all the answers you'll need. We have everything go through him."

The coach never called me.

Those coaches will promise parents that their sons will get to play against the most talented high school players in the country, they'll get to take some memorable trips, and then the coach will get the son a college scholarship — he says. And on the other end, they are promising a college coach somewhere that they can deliver this kid.

Two highly respected college coaches, Jack Bruen of Colgate and Bobby Cremins of Georgia Tech, have told me they are alarmed over the problem, and that it is a nightmare in New York City. I have heard of cases where high school players have missed their school's championship game because they were off somewhere playing for an AAU coach. The problem was the subject of a feature story in *Sports Illustrated* in July 1997.

There are cases where AAU coaches have gotten jobs as assistant coaches of college teams through these connections. Parents should be aware of these unscrupulous characters. They are street merchants of the lowest kind, flesh peddlers who are willing to risk a young athlete's future just to advance their own secret agendas.

Adrian Dantley did everything the right way. The result was a list of six schools he wanted to visit: Maryland, Minnesota, North Carolina, North Carolina State, Notre Dame and Southern California. He told me at the outset that he wanted to go away to college, which would eliminate Maryland, but Lefty kept pouring on his charm, and Adrian began to wonder if he should change his mind. But no, he told me later, he was going away, and would I mind calling Lefty and telling him? I said I'd be happy to call him the next day.

Adrian called me at home the following evening, talking in a very low voice, and asked if I had called Lefty yet. I told him I hadn't gotten to it that day, but it was on my list of things to do the next morning.

Then Adrian says, "Well, don't call him yet."

"Why?"

"Because," he whispered, "he's over here with a Maryland uniform with my name and number on it, and a warmup jacket with my name on that, too."

That uniform gimmick almost worked, but Adrian decided to go away to school after all and made his mark at Notre Dame and in the NBA. His preference to leave home is the only reason that Maryland wasn't able to add Adrian to a lineup that included John Lucas, Len Elmore and Tom McMillan.

*When the Cleveland Cavaliers used the DeMatha gym
for a practice session in 1992, Danny Ferry, his
former star, took time out to visit with Morgan.*

Danny Ferry got the chance to become an All-American at Duke and a star with the Cleveland Cavaliers by making the most of his great potential as a student-athlete, and by deciding, along with his parents, to follow our guidelines in handling the recruiting pressures in his senior year.

If any parent had the qualifications to say he was going to ignore our recruiting guidelines and handle his son's situation himself, it was Danny Ferry's father. Here's a man who was a college All-American basketball player himself at St. Louis University, a star in the NBA and general manager of the Washington Bullets when they won their only championship in 1978. He was still the Bullets' GM when Danny came to DeMatha in 1980.

Their father did the same with Danny that he did with Bob Jr. He followed our system and our guidelines, both the letter and the spirit. He and his wife, Rita, were smart enough to know that if you have put your son or daughter in the right situation, the best thing you can do next is stay out of their way and let your child grow. Let the coach do his job. Our system worked for Bob, who became a high school standout and then captain of his team at Harvard. There was every reason to believe that the same system would work for Danny, too.

In my eight years of coaching Bob and Danny Ferry, I never received one phone call from either of their parents. Bob Sr. never told me how to handle his sons, never said I should do something different, never questioned what position either son was playing. With all of his qualifications, the only things Bob Ferry Sr. did during his sons' eight years at DeMatha was to drive them fifty miles roundtrip to school every day and come to their games to cheer for them.

After seeing our guidelines work for Bob Jr., their father knew how to respond when the college recruiters started to call him about Danny. Because Bob Sr. was an NBA executive, his phone number was public information. The college scouts could just call the Bullets' offices at Capital Centre and talk to him there. But when they did and they told Bob that their college was interested in Bob Jr. or Danny, he always said, "That's wonderful. Just call Morgan. Everything goes through the coach's office."

Both boys followed our guidelines perfectly. In Danny's case, he narrowed his list of schools to Maryland, Duke, North Carolina and Virginia. Then he eliminated Virginia. After he made his final decision — it must be the player's decision and nobody else's — we called a news conference to take place in the DeMatha library.

Danny and I were walking through the gym together on our way to the library when he asked me, "Don't you want to know what my decision is?"

"No," I said, "because if you tell me now and some reporter asks me before the news conference starts, I'll have to tell him what I know. This way, I can honestly say I don't know."

The library had so many reporters, newspaper photographers and TV camera crews in it that it looked as if Danny were running for mayor. When the big moment came and he revealed that he was going to Duke, it was news to me.

I followed the same system and the same guidelines with my own sons. Brendan and Joe were both good students as well as good basketball players, so both received scholarship offers. Brendan was offered a scholarship by Virginia Military Institute — VMI — plus Randolph-Macon and Roanoke College. He visited those three schools and Virginia and Yale.

Then he decided he wanted to visit the University of Pennsylvania, too. Penn turned out to be the college of his choice. After completing his first two years, when he played on Penn's junior varsity basketball team, he dropped himself from the basketball program, concentrated on his degree and is now a senior vice president of a successful Wall Street brokerage firm.

Joe was recruited by Western Maryland College. Two other schools, Saint Joseph's and LaSalle, expressed an interest in him. Both schools are in Philadelphia, so Joe visited them and also made campus trips to Loyola of Baltimore, the University of Virginia and James Madison University in Harrisonburg, Virginia.

Joe chose Maryland. He played one year of college basketball before injuring his shoulder, but he made sure to get himself a solid education and a degree. Today he is my assistant coach at DeMatha.

In both cases, and with our daughters, Cathy, Tricia and Carol, I made certain to follow my own advice to other parents over the years. Kathy and I advised all five of our children on the question of where to go to college, because it is one of the two or three most important decisions they will ever make. But that's the key: They will make the decisions, not their parents.

Kathy and I listened, advised, suggested and asked. But we never told them where to go to college or what their major should be, just as we never told them what boy or girl to marry or where to work. It's their lives, and they have the right to live them by themselves. Some parents — fortunately only some — try to live their children's lives for them, but that's both unfair and unwise. If the school you told them to attend proves to be the wrong one for them, or if the one you told them to marry turns out to be incompatible, or if the career field they entered because you wanted them to is one they are not suited for, they may never forgive you.

If you try to impose your will on your children as they consider the critical questions of college, career, marriage and others, you will stunt their growth and close their minds, two of the worst offenses we could possibly commit against our children. To try to dictate to them as they consider these decisions creates the very real danger that you might bankrupt your children in every way — morally, intellectually and even financially.

Instead, we can follow the advice of another parent, Harry Truman:

> "If you want to be a good parent, find out what your children want to do. If it's decent and honorable, advise them to do it."

Seven

Socrates told the people of ancient Athens, "Things of great value come only after hard work." That is the kind of wisdom that made Socrates one of the greatest teachers in the history of the world. It is also the kind of attitude that breeds success as individuals, as sports teams and as a nation.

The enemy of this philosophy is something we never used to hear about, a term not used until recent years, called "instant gratification," whose supporters have an attitude directly opposite that taught by Socrates. Its champions say, "Never mind all that talk about working hard and paying the price. We want ours handed to us, and we want it now."

105

Fortunately, this is not the philosophy of the majority, at least not yet. But coaches, teachers, employers, parents and others see enough of it to know that already the number of people with this attitude is cause for concern. Most of the parents who subscribe to this philosophy as the one which is best for their children feel this way for only the most noble of reasons — because they want what they think is best for their kids, and they want it for them as soon as possible.

However, this parental attitude is at least counter-productive and at times downright harmful. Their kids end up achieving less while wanting more and sometimes are hurt by their parents' search for instant gratification for their sons and daughters.

Every coach has had parents come up to him or her and ask for some assurance that Johnny or Jane will be able to skip the freshman team and go directly to playing on the junior varsity, or skip the jayvee and play on the varsity. They want to know how many minutes he will be able to play, and whether he will be able to play his favorite position. It's the high school version of what we see at the professional level — players demanding guaranteed contracts lasting six and seven years, plus a seven-figure signing bonus up front. Get all you can, and get it guaranteed, and get as much of it now as possible.

That sends the wrong message to all of us, students and adults. It says that you can have instant money, instant success, instant gratification. But life isn't like that, and our kids need to understand this. Life does not provide instant gratification. Except in the rarest of cases, the world just doesn't work that way, and we parents, teachers and coaches need to make certain that our kids understand this, accept it and are willing to work within these ground rules.

The father of an eighth grade student contacted me in the spring of 1996 to talk about his son and the possibility that he might apply for admission to DeMatha. He said his son was a basketball player. I said fine, that we'd be happy to welcome him if he passes the entrance exam given each year by the Archdiocese of Washington, and if he wanted to, he could then try out for one of our basketball teams, just like any other member of our student body.

The father wanted more than that for his son. He wanted guarantees, but I told him I couldn't give him any. The father said another school "will guarantee he'll make the jayvee in the ninth grade."

I told him just the opposite. "I can't make any guarantee," I said. "All I can guarantee is that your son will be allowed to try out for the team. If he makes it, then we'll let him play where it is best for the team and for him. It's not him first and then the team. It's the team first. We'll consider his overall development and what's best for him, freshman or junior varsity. After his freshman year, we'll watch him and decide whether he should play on the jayvee or varsity."

The boy did not enroll at DeMatha.

It reminded me of Lincoln's advice to parents. He said that any time we do something for our children that they should be doing for themselves, we weaken them. I have always tried to be honest with our own children and those entrusted to my care as a coach and a teacher. I have always been determined that our kids and any other kids and their parents would never be able to point a finger at me twenty years later and be able to say, "You cheated me. You didn't let me grow, and you didn't let me make my own mistakes and learn from them and pick myself up and go on."

That's one reason I've always leveled with any young person under my care by saying to them, "I'm not going to tell you what you want to hear, because ninety percent of the world will do that. I'm going to tell you what you need to hear."

At the same time that the young man's father was seeking guarantees from me before the '96-97 season, we had two promising sophomores who could have made our varsity team, but they would not have played much because they were not as good as the players who would be part of our substitution rotation. On the other hand, they could play jayvee ball as tenth graders, get a considerable amount of playing time and be ready for two years of varsity ball as juniors and seniors.

I put it to them on that basis. They both had the same reaction. They passed up the opportunity to get the in-

Basketball Hall of Fame Photo

Morgan Wootten expresses his appreciation for winning the John W. Bunn Award from the Basketball Hall of Fame in 1991.

stant gratification of being on the varsity and being able to tell their families and friends that they were varsity athletes even though they were only in the tenth grade. Instead, they told me in so many words, "Coach, we know you'll do what's best for us. We've never been in this situation before, but you deal with it every year, so we'll do what you suggest."

They played on the jayvee as tenth graders in the 1996-97 season. They played most of every game, became excellent junior varsity players and are now ready to compete as varsity athletes. From my years of experience, I can tell you right now what any experienced coach could tell you: Both of those boys will be successful high school basketball players, they will have more fun because they are better now than they would be if they had sat on the bench all last season, and — this is the best part — they both will win scholarships to college.

For both of those deserving boys, the sky's the limit — because they resisted the temptation to try for instant gratification and instead chose the old-fashioned way. In the words of the television commercial of a few years ago, "They earned it." Socrates would be proud of those two boys. So am I.

♦ ♦ ♦

An anonymous coach in Canada once composed a set of "Ten Commandments" for parents of school-age children. I've tried to follow them myself over the years as a father. I list them here as recommended reading — make that required reading — for every mother and father:

1. Make sure your child knows that, win or lose, scared or heroic, you love him or her, appreciate their efforts and are not disappointed in them.

2. Try your best to be completely honest about your child's athletic capability, his competitive attitude, his sportsmanship, and his actual skill level.

3. Be helpful, but don't coach him on the way to the rink, track or court, or on the way back, or at breakfast.

4. Teach him to enjoy the thrill of competition. Don't say, "Winning doesn't count," because it does.

5. And hear this, parents: Try not to relive your athletic life through your child in a way that creates pressure. Don't pressure him because of your pride.

6. Don't compete with the coach. Remember, in many cases the coach becomes a hero to his athletes, a person who can do no wrong.

7. Don't compare the skill, courage or attitudes of your child with that of other members of the team, at least not in his hearing.

8. You should also get to know the coach so you can be sure his philosophy, attitudes, ethics and

knowledge are such that you are happy to expose your child to him.

9. Always remember that children tend to exaggerate, both when praised and when criticized. Temper your reactions when your children bring home tales of woe, or heroics.

10. Make a point of understanding courage and the fact that it is relative. Some of us climb mountains but fear a fight. Some of us fight but turn to jelly if a bee buzzes nearby. A child must know: Courage is not absence of fear, but rather it is doing something in spite of fear.

There is a gold mine of good advice for parents in that list. All of us mothers and fathers should heed the wisdom of that anonymous coach and be thankful that, whoever he is and wherever he is, he took the time to compose these Ten Commandments and pass them on to us.

Notice that the commandments do not say anything about being entitled to instant gratification. On the contrary, they emphasize "the thrill of competition" and the important role that winning can play in our lives. Whoever that coach was clearly knew what every other coach knows — that trying to grab too much too soon can thwart your child's development later. Athletes who develop at an even pace during their growing-up years often become much better players than those who got too much too soon.

In many cases, they do much better in sports, and in life, than the early achievers.

Those who become dominant stars at an early age get there because their talent level is so high or because they are so much bigger than the others, but they have poor work habits because they see that they don't have to work as hard as their teammates to be successful. They're already good. But those poor work habits catch up with them later, and by high school age you frequently see others outpacing those who were stars in the fifth and sixth grades.

One of our most important roles as parents is to be a resource for our children so they know they can come to us for advice and information while also knowing that we won't tell them what to do or try to relive our lives through them. We can suggest what to do, and what not to do, but our kids must be able to feel by the time they reach high school that we are a helpful resource as supportive and proud parents.

High school students must also understand that they have certain responsibilities of their own, especially where getting their education is concerned. All five of our children went to college, and Kathy and I were happy to pay their tuition and room and board. But we also wanted them to feel that they had a stake themselves in their educations, so we made them pay for the cost of their books and provide their own spending money. Anybody who came up short would have to mow a few more lawns or wait on a few more tables. No exceptions.

It happened in the case of our daughter, Cathy. She got a job as a waitress in Ocean City, Maryland, an Atlantic Ocean beach resort which is popular with residents of the Washington area. We thought the experience of living away from home for a summer, supporting herself and saving for her next year of college would be a valuable learning experience for her, and it was — but her learning continued after she moved back home at the end of the summer.

She discovered she had not saved enough, so she hit me up for the money she needed to pay for her books and living expenses for the new college year. I gently refused. When she asked again, I reminded her, "Cathy, a deal is a deal. Mom and I pay your tuition and your room and board. You pay for your books and expenses. It's always been that way."

When she said she didn't know where she could get the money, I offered a simple solution: "I guess you'll have to wait on a few more tables."

That's exactly what she did. She got a part-time job at a restaurant near our neighborhood and saved until she had what she needed.

Our daughter, Tricia, took a different approach, and that one worked, too. She began her higher education at a two-

Morgan Wootten outlines strategy during a timeout in the late 1980s, with son Brendan (second from left) listening.

year college while working part-time jobs, ones she might not have been able to get if she had been a full-time student at a four-year college. She worked in year-round jobs, some of them full-time, for a video production firm, *USA TODAY* and on Capitol Hill. Today she is on the professional staff of our county's Prince George's Community College while also working on her master's degree.

Brendan was the toughest negotiator of them all in those arrangements for financial assistance. On Easter vacation during his freshman year at Penn, he came home and told me that after a year there, he thought he deserved a raise in helping me with the annual mailings for our summer basketball camp. It was a legitimate point, so I quadrupled his salary — from $2.50 an hour (remember, this was ten years ago) to ten dollars.

Carol, our daughter, could tell Brendan got his raise. When she walked into the room where Brendan was stuffing envelopes, he was dancing as he stuffed.

The newest form of instant gratification is the growing number of high school athletes who are leap-frogging over college and going directly into the pros at age eighteen. In the case of tennis players, the situation is downright alarming, with little girls — and that's what they are — becoming professional athletes at age fourteen.

It doesn't make any difference how tall they are. In the more important definition, they are still little kids. Those who turn pro immediately out of high school, or even in the eighth or ninth grade in the case of tennis players, frequently at the urging of their parents, suddenly are thrust into the full-time company of athletes much older than they are. These men and women — not boys or girls — who have been around, who have a different lifestyle than anything these kids have been exposed to, who are earning tons more money, who have a tempting amount of spare time on their hands between games or tournaments, can have a profound impact on these kids, for better or for worse.

Imagine a seventeen-year-old basketball player who comes out of high school and immediately joins the company of players who are five and ten years older, even in their thirties. The kids are exposed right away to unbelievable pressures on the court and off, they receive instant recognition and even god-like status, and they have more money being thrown at them in playing contracts and endorsements than they could imagine because of their youth and lack of experience or knowledge.

Those kids who jump right out of high school into the pros are cutting four or five years out of their lives, as much as one-third in the case of a fifteen-year-old. That would be equal to a forty-five-year-old person taking fifteen years out of his life. Is that a good idea? Obviously not. No sane person would even suggest such a thing.

Professional basketball is in a unique position in this problem. Even though I have problems with kids turning pro early, those who do it in tennis at age fourteen or fifteen have a lot of company, because so many other kids at that age do the same thing. Likewise in professional baseball. A lot of players go into the minor leagues right out of high school. But professional basketball poses more of a problem because there are so few players in the National Basketball Association who are only seventeen or eighteen years old.

A look at the record shows that only a very few teenagers who skipped college and went directly into the NBA ever made it big. Some people point to Moses Malone as one who did, but Moses played the first years of his career in the old ABA, the American Basketball Association. As a result, when he eventually began to compete with the big boys in the NBA, he already had several years of professional experience under his belt.

Most of the kids who skip college make a common mistake, and it inevitably leads to their downfall: They start listening to the wrong people. They are surrounded by entourages of four, five or six "friends" who advise them on what decisions to make, what to do with their money and what deals to make. In many cases, the members of the entourage are the kids they grew up with, so maybe it's a case of the athlete trying to bring his social life with him into the NBA and into his strange new adult world.

The danger is that those "friends" will find every way imaginable to dispose of the player's money. In far too many cases, the athlete will find himself broke. I don't care how many millions they get in a signing bonus and how many more millions they earn every year — the landscape of every professional sport history is littered with the sad, even tragic, memories of such documented cases where the player ended up broke and even declaring bankruptcy to get out from under massive amounts of debt.

It's tragic to witness, and I have. It happened to a prominent high school player in the Washington area. He started college, but he never finished. He left early, became a big-bucks player in the NBA and is broke today. He made the mistake of listening to the wrong people. In his case, most of his decisions were made for him by his father, who told his son where to go to college and then advised him when to turn pro and what kind of a deal to accept.

All of that might have worked, although I doubt it, but the odds were stacked even higher against this young man because his father was completely unqualified for the role he assumed. How could he advise his son on what college to go to? The father had never been to college himself. How could he advise his son on when to turn pro? He had never been a professional athlete. And how could he advise him on the deal the pros were offering? He wasn't a lawyer or an accountant or an agent. The result was sadly predictable.

A fundamental question in the case of every young athlete, successful or unsuccessful, is: To whom am I listening? Am I listening to the people who are telling me what I want to hear? Or am I listening to people who have a track record on the subject? Did the people telling me what college to attend ever go to college themselves? Were the people advising me on my career professional athletes themselves? Are the people who are advising me on what to do with my money bankers or brokers or investors themselves?

In my own lifetime, I can remember the sad story of one of the first professional athletes who lost all of his money, and he made tons of it — Joe Louis. Too many people found ways to get his money. Maybe nobody ever did anything illegal, but the fact is that Louis, with all the money he made as the heavyweight champion of the world for so many years, and a highly popular champion back in the days when heavyweight champion of the world really meant something, ended up broke.

How about the people around Louis? He always had an entourage of people around him. Did they end up broke? I can make a pretty good guess. Members of the entourages are bloodsuckers. They always find a way to get the athlete's money for themselves, and the athlete, as a result, runs out of money. Any time I see a professional athlete with a big entourage around him when he arrives to give a talk at a basketball clinic or shows up at a television studio for an interview, I say to myself, "There's a guy who's going to end up broke." Why? Because nobody can afford an entourage.

There's an old saying in the navy: "Who has the admiral's ear?" That's a critical question for every player of every sport in high school and college today who hopes for a future as a professional athlete. Who has your ear?

How can young athletes avoid this fate? Go to college. Get a sound education. And make sure you're listening to the right people, people who are qualified to advise you and who don't have their hands in your pocket.

This does not apply, of course, if your ambition is simply to make all the money you can. Then go ahead and turn pro at whatever age you feel like it. But before you do, you have to ask yourself: Is all this money going to make me happy? You have to make that call. Consider all the stories you have heard or read about people with piles of money who have never found happiness, who ended up divorced, in many cases even dead from substance abuse or something else, simply because they had all the money in the world but were still not happy.

There used to be a rule in professional basketball that a high school player could not enter the NBA until the year his college class graduated. They did away with that rule. Why? Because the NBA is such big business now, like every other professional sport. The leaders of the NBA are going to do whatever is good for their business. There's too much money involved now, for the owners, the players, the sponsors, the television networks and for the NBA itself. But if we are ever to solve this problem of kids who

Values vs. Instant Gratification

© Disney

Coach Pat Riley of the Miami Heat presents Morgan Wootten with the 1991 award from the Walt Disney Company as Sports Coach of the Year as part of Disney's annual American Teacher Awards.

are clearly too young to become pros in the NBA, that rule must be reinstated. And it would not be a bad idea to establish the same rule for baseball and football, too.

With such a rule, the young athletes would get more of an education — in their social lives as well as in the classroom — even if they did not receive their degrees. They would be far more mature physically, mentally, emotionally, educationally and socially. As a direct result, they would be much more prepared to face what is a demanding life anyhow as a professional athlete.

Another easy yet effective step would be for professional sports to require that athletes who skip college must take certain minimal courses in the off-season to remain eligible, even if it's something as fundamental as how to balance your checkbook. Most of the high school kids who skip college have never had an opportunity to learn something that basic. That's just one example of the countless features of life as an adult that they have to learn somewhere from somebody. If they are not going to learn these things in college and summer jobs and elsewhere in the way all other high school graduates continue to learn about life in the adult world, then they should be required to take these basic courses.

Another requirement which I suggest is worthy of consideration would be to earmark a certain percentage of the salary of a kid skipping college and put it in an escrow account, to be held there until he receives a degree, even if it's only from a two-year community college, or until he retires from his career as a professional athlete.

When kids fresh out of high school enter the world of the professional athlete at age seventeen or eighteen, they encounter many unsavory characters who chase after the pros — the women who follow the professional teams in every sport, the financial bloodsuckers, and others. Four years on a college campus — four more years of growing up as a person — will go a long way toward preparing an athlete for coping with his or her new life.

The NBA has tried to slow things down a bit by imposing a salary cap on rookies. Teams can pay them only three million dollars a year for three years — only three million! — and then they must become free agents.

Then they can sign with another team for still more money. It reminds me of a classic comment by Senator Everett Dirksen of Illinois, the Republican party's late senate leader, who once characterized all the money in budget legislation by saying, "A billion here and a billion there and pretty soon you're talking about big money." The same goes for the NBA salary cap. It's a noble idea on the surface, but — three million here and three million there and pretty soon you're talking about big money.

The high school star should ask himself or herself if they would want to skip college if the money were removed from the equation. The question would become: If I had to play for only fifty thousand dollars a year instead of millions, would I still want to do it? Obviously, the answer in almost every case will be no. That exercise then tells the athlete they're doing it simply for the money — positively no other reason. And that's risky, because the chances are that all the millions by themselves still won't make the athlete happy, for all the reasons cited above.

High school athletes, and those in college who are thinking about leaving early so they can turn pro, then are faced with the most fundamental question of all: Is money going to rule my life. Will it determine all the decisions I make in life?

And athletes are not alone in having to make that decision. People in all walks of life have to decide the same thing. I know. I've done it. That was precisely the decision I was faced with in considering that fantastic offer from North Carolina State. Seven hundred thousand dollars, plus free college educations for all five of my children? You can imagine how tempted I was, and this was almost twenty years ago.

Buck Offutt put the whole question in its clearest form when he told me to remove the money from the equation and then see if I were still interested in the offer. Then the decision was easy. And my life has been immeasurably happier. I have been able to continue enjoying my home town, my family and life-long friendships. I have had the uniquely happy experience of coaching my two sons, of seeing our children succeed in college and become happy husbands and wives and parents, of bouncing our grand-children on my knee any day I want to, and of being home for birthdays and anniversaries that I might have missed otherwise. And I have never once missed that seven hundred thousand dollars.

As our children went through their high school and college years, I occasionally reminded myself that our lives with them become a collection of memories, which raises an important question for parents: What do you want your kids, and yourself, to be able to remember about your years together at home and your role in helping them past their milestones? If instant gratification for your son or daughter is so important to you, it will be to him or her, too. If playing a few more minutes is going to determine whether your son or daughter are happy, or whether playing shortstop instead of left field is the most important thing in your life, then your life is badly out of balance. His will be, too, and your memories in later years won't be nearly as rewarding and heartwarming as they might have been.

After all, whether we are coaches, teachers, parents or — in my case — all three, we have to ask ourselves periodically the most fundamental question of all:

Which is more important — for our son or daughter to become a world-class athlete, or a world-class human being?

Eight

Chances are you've never heard of Patrick McGettigan or Eric Mitchell or Bill Collins. They aren't sports stars, not any more, but they are at the top of their professions every bit as much as Michael Jordan or Cal Ripken or Tiger Woods.

In addition to their high level of success, they have at least two other characteristics in common: They out-worked everyone else along the way, and they never gave in to anything. Winston Churchill would have loved all three of them.

Pat McGettigan is a high school graduate, an ex-Marine and was a seventeen-year employee with Blue Cross and Blue Shield, the health insurance giant, until 1982. That's

127

when he established Landmark Systems Corporation. Today Pat is still the head of Landmark, and it is now a forty-five million dollar international computer software company.

His future didn't look nearly that bright in 1952, thirty years before he founded Landmark. His mother had brought him to us at St. Joseph's Home for Boys, the orphanage where I was just starting what turned out, much to my later surprise, to be a coaching and teaching career. Pat still remembers everything about those days and those times. He reminisced about them in a two-page typewritten letter that he sent to me on July 12, 1996, while I was still unconscious after my liver transplant.

"Like many of the other kids," Pat wrote, "I was there because I came from a broken home and the poverty and abuse that went with it. Like so many of the kids in my neighborhood, I had started down a tough road, having flunked the third grade, and had many near misses on the streets. My mother always said she sent me there because she couldn't afford me, but I think the truth was more like keeping me out of reform school."

Pat told me he remembered watching our CYO football team at practice one afternoon early in his stay at Saint Joseph's, when he was still only a skinny eleven-year-old boy with no sports experience. He found our practice interesting to watch, so he stood there, looking out at the field from the sideline.

"It was at that point," Pat wrote in his letter, "where that critical first fork in the road took place." He reminded me that I "came over and said one simple sentence: 'Do you want to play?'"

That was the team that won the CYO championship, with Pat as one of our players. "I've often wondered," he wrote, "just how much I owe to experiencing that city champion Saint Joe's team, of learning how it felt to overcome adversity, of learning how to never give up, and most of all, how it felt to win in life."

Pat has applied his lessons from the football field to the rest of his life. "...regardless of whether I was afraid or behind by seventy points," he wrote, speaking about his career and his business ventures in sports terms, "my attitude in the last minute of play was always the same: Never give up!"

Then he said something that made my day when I read his letter several days after regaining consciousness. "Given everything that has happened," he wrote, "I thought it long overdue that I said, "Thanks, Morgan, for asking me, 'Do you want to play?'"

◆ ◆ ◆

Eric Mitchell — Dr. Eric Mitchell — came up to me before one of our basketball games when he was a tenth grader at DeMatha and asked me if he could take some pictures during our games for our school newspaper, The Stagline. He had decent size, so I asked him if he would like to be a player instead of a photographer. When he said yes enthusiastically, I encouraged him to try out for our junior varsity team.

As fate would have it, Eric made the jayvee as a tenth grader and then played on our varsity team as both a junior and a senior. He grew to six feet, five inches by his senior year in 1967, was our second leading rebounder for the season and the leading rebounder for all teams in the Knights of Columbus tournament. We won our conference championship, the city title and the Knights of Columbus. Eric won something for himself, too — a full scholarship to Saint Joseph's in Philadelphia.

Two things about Eric always stood out to me at every stage of his development — his work ethic and his unswerving determination to reach his goal, whatever it might be at that point in his young life. Even his admission to DeMatha was an example. He was rejected when he applied as a freshman, so he came back as a sophomore and applied again. This time he was accepted. Then he tried out for the jayvee basketball team, and some of his friends told him he would never make it, but he did. Then they told him he would never make the varsity, but he did, and he became a star. Then they said he would never win a scholarship to college, but he did that, too.

At college, Eric continued to defy the doubters. They said he would not be able to play college basketball and carry a heavy academic load at the same time, especially since he wanted to take a pre-med curriculum so he could become a doctor. But he did.

His coach called me during Eric's first year of basketball at Saint Joseph's and asked me if I thought he could handle the combined load of academics and a demanding sports schedule. I told him Eric's history of always achieving his goals and showing the doubters they were wrong. "Believe me," I said, "if Eric says he can do it, he can do it." And he did. He was a successful student while also being a successful college athlete.

After graduating from Saint Joseph's, Eric wanted to enter the University of Pennsylvania medical school. He asked me to write a letter of recommendation for him. By that time his academic record spoke for itself, but just in case, I made sure to say, "If this is what Eric wants to do, he'll be the best."

That's exactly what he is. Today he is a nationally known authority in orthopedic surgery and sport medicine. And when President Clinton dispatched emergency assistance to the troubled island of Haiti, the head of the U.S. public health team was Dr. Eric Mitchell.

Bill Collins had all the same basic characteristics as Patrick McGettigan and Eric Mitchell, but, like them, he had some of his own, too. Two special things I remember about Bill were: He was always prepared, and he never worried about trying to be better than someone else. Instead, he concentrated his time and energies on being the best that he could be.

I saw Bill — he was Billy back then — in the eighth grade. By the time he came to DeMatha, he was developing into an outstanding catcher in baseball and a terrific quarterback in football. He became DeMatha's starting catcher for three years and stepped into the quarterback's job after our starter was injured and threw three touchdown passes to lead DeMatha to a thrilling upset victory over a team of our conference's all-stars.

Bill was always prepared. Like Pat and Eric and James Brown and Adrian Dantley and Danny Ferry and all the other star athletes who have come out of DeMatha in so many different sports, Bill had an outstanding work ethic. He worked hard in practice, he kept himself in tip-top physical condition, he learned as much as he could about our next opponent's strengths and weaknesses and their tendencies, and he paid attention to his coaches and followed their advice. He was "coachable," one of the most basic qualities that every coach values in any athlete.

Bill's willingness to concentrate on what he could be without worrying about what others might achieve is undoubtedly one of the ingredients that has contributed to his phenomenal success in the business world. He has been a winner at every turn of his life because, among other reasons, he never asked how much he was going to play, he never compared himself to others, and he always worked his hardest to develop his abilities to their full potential.

I have always advised my players against comparing themselves to others, a mistake many people make in life. I call it a "mistake" because it is a waste of your time and is even counter-productive. You cannot control how good someone else is or how well they do in school or in their work. I have always reminded my players and my students, "The only thing you can control is how good you will be. Never try to be better than someone else. But, never cease to be the best that you can be." The Army recruiting slogan applies to civilians too, of all ages: "Be all that you can be."

Bill went to George Washington University on a baseball scholarship. After graduation, he became a professional baseball player with a term in the minor leagues. In the early days of the paging industry, he formed First Page, one of the first companies in that field. Today he is a multi-millionaire as president and CEO of Metrocall. He's something else, too — the leader of a group of investors working to bring major league baseball back to Washington. He may not be a household name yet, but he will be sooner or later, when he stands next to the President of the United States and watches him throw out the first ball as

Bill's team, the one he will own, plays its first game.

Those of us who know Bill Collins have come to expect such things from him.

Adrian Dantley was like Eric Mitchell. He proved a lot of people wrong on his road to first one success and then another. I had an early insight into Adrian's make-up that told me he could turn out to be a special person. On Christmas afternoon of his freshman year at DeMatha, there was a knock on the front door of our home. When I opened it, there was Adrian. He asked, "Coach, can I borrow the key to the gym? I'd like to practice my shooting."

It reminded me of the Princeton student who used to come by Saint John's High School one summer ten years earlier, when Joe Gallagher and I were operating our Metropolitan Boys Basketball Camp. He'd shoot and shoot and shoot, alone in the gym, every evening on his way home from his job as a summer intern on Capitol Hill.

That dedication, what coaches call the willingness to "pay the price," produced dividends for that college student at every step of his career. He became a basketball All-American at Princeton, and Joe and I have always liked to think that all those thousands and thousands of shots by himself in the Saint John's gym helped. Then he became a star in the NBA with the New York Knicks. When his long and successful professional basketball career was over, he got a job on Capitol Hill again — as Senator Bill Bradley of New Jersey.

Basketball Hall of Fame Photo

Bob Kurland, a member of the Basketball Hall of Fame and its president in 1991, presents that year's John W. Bunn Award to Morgan Wootten for outstanding contributions to basketball.

As a ninth grader on that Christmas afternoon, Adrian was a big kid but a pudgy one, so people said he would never be a success as a high school basketball player. He became an All-Metropolitan player, meaning one of the best in the Washington area, and a high school All-American. Many college coaches rated him the best high school basketball player in America.

But the skeptics said he would never make it big in college because he was too heavy and too slow, he wasn't quick enough and he couldn't shoot from the outside and, oh, one more thing — he was too small, only six feet, five inches. With every college in the nation to choose from, Adrian selected Notre Dame for two reasons — its academic reputation and the national exposure he would get by playing on a nationally ranked team against a tough schedule of opponents on network television and in postseason play.

Adrian never made any bones about it — his ambition was to make it to the National Basketball Association and then become a star. After he enrolled at Notre Dame, he fooled the skeptics again. He made the freshman All-American team, and remained an All-American as a sophomore and a junior. Then he hooked up with his DeMatha teammate, Kenny Carr, to win the Gold Medal in basketball for the U.S. at the 1976 Olympics. Adrian was the U.S. team's leading scorer.

Kenny had the same competitive drive as Adrian. He

banged up his knee as a sophomore, and the doctors said Kenny might never be able to play basketball again. Kenny worked hard all summer, defied the odds and the doctors' prediction and kept right on going — a star for us in his senior year of high school and the same kind of success at North Carolina State. Then, even with back injuries and more knee problems, he played in the NBA for ten seasons. With two players blessed with both the abilities and the attitudes of Adrian Dantley and Kenny Carr, no wonder the United States won the '76 Gold Medal.

After the Olympics, Adrian headed for the NBA, and the skeptics persisted. All that success at the college level was nice, even impressive, they conceded, but he would not make it in the pros. He may have been able to get by at the college level, but this was the NBA. He would have to be even quicker and stronger.

He was. He was voted the Rookie of the Year with Buffalo. He won the league's scoring championship twice, was an All-Star seven times, played in the NBA for fifteen years and scored over 23,000 points.

All of these athletes in these success stories agreed with that wise old saying, "Success is a journey, not a destination." They were extremely coachable, which made them the delight of any coach who ever had the pleasure of coaching them. And they responded well to motivation, in addition to being self-motivators.

When Adrian left for his freshman year at Notre Dame

in 1973, he took along his copy of a poem I distribute to
my players. It stresses the need to be a good role model
for those younger athletes who look up to them and will
emulate them as they become high school and college athletes themselves. The last stanza of that poem says:

> You are setting an example
> Every day in all you do,
> For the little boy who's waiting
> To grow up to be like you.

All DeMatha players and the kids at our summer basketball camps receive a variety of such motivational
messages in materials which I have used throughout my
coaching and teaching career, some of which I've written
myself. They are effective tools in reaching young men
and women today or in any other era. Things may change
from decade to decade, from generation to generation and,
in our case today, from century to century, but some attitudes and values should never change, and they don't in
our system of coaching and teaching — in touching lives.

For example, I emphasize loyalty to my players, my
coaching staff and the kids at our summer camps. In doing so, I quote one of the best descriptions of that virtue,
by Elbert Hubbard:

> If you work for a man, in heaven's name work
> for him: Speak well of him and stand by the
> institution he represents...Remember — an
> ounce of loyalty is worth a pound of

cleverness...If you must growl, condemn and eternally find fault, resign your position and when you are on the outside, damn to your heart's content...But as long as you are a part of the institution, do not condemn it...If you do, the first high wind that comes along will blow you away, and probably you will never know why.

Another characteristic which I have always emphasized is class — conducting yourself in a professional and dignified manner, dressing the right way for the occasion, using the proper kind of speech and acting always with professionalism and integrity, two words we don't hear often enough any more. I distribute this description of class:

- ◆ Class never runs scared. It is surefooted and confident. It can handle whatever comes along.
- ◆ Class has a sense of humor. It knows that a good laugh is the best lubricant for oiling the machinery of human relations.
- ◆ Class never makes excuses. It takes its lumps and learns from past mistakes. Class knows that good manners are nothing more than a series of petty sacrifices.
- ◆ Class bespeaks an aristocracy that has nothing to do with money. Some extremely wealthy people have no class at all, while others who are struggling to make ends meet are loaded with it.

- Class is real. You can't fake it.
- The person with class makes everyone feel comfortable because he is comfortable with himself.
- If you have class, you've got it made. If you don't have class, no matter what else you have, it doesn't make any difference.

Each year at the start of basketball practice, I distribute my own description of "The DeMatha Basketball Player:"

> A DeMatha basketball player is a man with pride in himself as a student, an athlete and a member of the community. He, as a member of the basketball program, not only represents himself and his family but also his teammates and coaches. As our program continues to grow and prosper, he will constantly be in the eye of his fellow students and the general public. He will be a leader and conduct himself in such a manner as to be praised, not as a basketball player, but more importantly as a man.

> A DeMatha basketball player has goals for himself as a student, player and a man. To attain those goals, he bases his lifestyle on hard work, one hundred percent effort, sacrifice, second effort, determination, punctuality and persistence. Just as these ideals will bring championships on the court, they will also reap rewards in the classroom and earn him

greater respect as an individual.

A DeMatha player always has his head up; he looks his fellow man and the world in the eye. He is a class man in a class program. A DeMatha player always has his priorities in the proper order: God first, family second, school and studies third.

Congratulations and welcome to the team.

There is another valuable message which I distribute to our players and to all the kids at our summer basketball camps. It's in the form of a poem, and it tells us how to conduct ourselves after success has propelled us into the public eye:

What is Fame?
Commonly a goal for many in life
is for all to know their name,
For them, their social circle is vast
and, for some, they learn of fame.

A thrilling experience. An awesome feeling.
One cannot deny this as true,
But is a daily dose of public inspection
really satisfying to you?

Do these people really know
what makes you especially rare?

Are those individuals there when needed
and do they really care?

Never let audiences or unknown souls
influence your beliefs or ideals,
For, in the end, if you weren't true to yourself
your life won't maintain its appeals.

So however life leads you throughout the years
to yourself be fair and true,
When the end is near
you'll have no fear
of wondering if you were good to you.

That poem has been a favorite of mine since the poet wrote it in 1989, when she was only twenty-one years old. I like it for two reasons: For its valuable and beautiful message, and because I know the poet personally. She is our daughter, Tricia.

Some people may say these things are corny, but successful people like Adrian Dantley and Eric Mitchell and James Brown and Bill Collins and Pat McGettigan don't think so. And on these virtues and characteristics and all the others we emphasize, not one person has ever disagreed with me.

There's another success story in the making right now, and his name will surprise people in Washington: Charles "Hawkeye" Whitney. My prediction will surprise them because Hawkeye is not in the kind of place that normally breeds success. He's in prison.

If his name sounds familiar, it is because he was a star basketball player at DeMatha, a high school All-American and one of the finest basketball players in the history of our school. In the mid-1970s, he was probably the most popular and respected high school player in the Washington area. He became a first team All-Atlantic Coast Conference star at North Carolina State and a young pro who was destined to make it in the NBA until he tore his knee up early in his second year.

In high school, he lived with his parents in a poor neighborhood of Southeast Washington, in a building where most of the apartment units were condemned. His parents were on welfare, both of them sickly people who became amputees and are now deceased.

Hawkeye was recommended to me by a junior high school coach. Before I ever saw him play, he was on a team that was in a tournament with our junior varsity team, so I told Marty Fletcher, the Denver University coach who was then our jayvee coach, to take a look at him for me.

Marty reported to me the next day that our jayvees had won their first game in the tournament. I asked him, "What about this kid Hawkeye?"

Marty said, "Oh, he's not bad. He's about six-three. He scored a lot of points. He's a pretty good player."

Shane Battier of Detroit County Day School in Beverly Hills, Michigan, receives the first annual Morgan Wootten Award as the McDonald's National High School Player of the Year for the 1996–97 season only six months after the coach's transplant.

After the next night, Marty told me our jayvees won again. Then I asked my same question: "How did Hawkeye do?"

Marty answered, "Well, his team won, too, so I'll get a chance to watch him again tomorrow in the next round. I told you he was about six-three, but he's a little taller, maybe about six-five. He's even better than I thought he was. He runs a little faster and jumps a little higher. He does a lot of things I didn't realize."

After one of the semi-final games, which Marty's jayvees won, I got his full report on our players. Then I asked my usual question: "How did Hawkeye do?"

Marty couldn't wait to tell me. "I'm going to tell you something, Morgan," he said. "He's about six-six, and he can rebound, he can score inside and out, he can do it all. He is something else. I had no idea he was that good. I'll be able to tell you more after tomorrow, because we're playing his team in the championship game."

The conversation after that game went like this:

"How'd it go last night, Marty?"

"Not too good. We got beaten pretty badly."

"That's too bad. How did Hawkeye look?"

"He's coming to DeMatha next year."

"Yeah, I know. But how did you know?"

"Because after the game, he came over to our bench and shook every single player's hand, and then he told everybody, 'Don't worry, fellas, because next year I'll be playing with you instead of against you, so don't worry about a thing. Everything will be all right.'"

"So how did he look?"

"How'd he look? He's seven-foot-two, and I've got news for you. From now on, everybody else is playing for second place. He's the best."

Charles had a brilliant career at DeMatha, and an equally successful career at N.C. State after receiving offers from almost every school in the country — Bobby Knight at Indiana and others — all of them wanted him.

After his stardom at N.C. State, he was selected in the first round of the NBA draft by the Kansas City Kings. Before he signed with the Kings, he came by DeMatha one day and showed me a new contract to endorse a brand of athletic shoes. The contract was for forty-five thousand dollars, more money than Hawkeye knew existed in the whole world, and a sizeable amount for anybody in the endorsement business in the late 1970s.

After a successful rookie season, he was playing in a game against the Milwaukee Bucks early in his second season when he unfortunately got "undercut," when another player accidentally cuts your legs out from under you. He virtually destroyed a knee, ending his career right there.

By Hawkeye's own admission, he drifted away from those people who had helped him to achieve success. In looking back, it seems clear that he lost his support group when he left DeMatha and began to listen instead to the "hangers-on" and the entourages. He ended up not just flat broke but also on drugs. No matter how many times he came back, with help from many of us who had known and loved him at DeMatha and other stops in his life, he kept slipping again. I tried to help him on several occasions. So did Mike Brey, the coach at the University of Delaware who was his DeMatha teammate. Others did, too.

He reached bottom in early 1996 when a drug dealer demanded that Hawkeye pay him what he owed him "or your sister is going to suffer." With that warning, Hawkeye accompanied the dealer on a night mission to rob somebody by forcing their victim at gunpoint to withdraw money from an automatic teller machine.

They found their victim at the subway station at National Airport, which isn't really a subway at that point because it is above ground. For their victim they chose a prosperous and successful-looking target, a man who was obviously a professional person. They had no way of knowing that the man they picked out was Hillary Clinton's lawyer, on his way home after spending all day with his client before the grand jury investigating the Whitewater case.

They drove him around all night, withdrew money out

of an ATM machine and released him the next morning. The news accounts said Hawkeye kept reassuring their victim that nothing was going to happen to him and then gave him twenty dollars for cab fare home when the episode was over. In the end, the victim got to go home, the drug dealer got his money, and the only one who didn't get anything was Hawkeye, who was then facing a prison term.

That's where he is today, in North Carolina. He has three more years before he will be released. When he is, he will become a success all over again. Why do I say that? For two reasons:

1. He has been a success before, so he can be again.
2. He is now a man with a mission, and it's the right kind of mission.

In his letters to me, which he sends every couple of weeks, and our two or three telephone conversations every month, Hawkeye repeatedly says he wants to preach his own gospel, especially to young people, after his release from prison. He wants to devote his time and his talents to telling people, "Don't make the mistakes I made. Don't use drugs. Don't surround yourself with an entourage. The people in it will get all your money. Don't surround yourself with people who will use you and abuse you. Remember who the people were who helped you on your way up the ladder and use those people, not the other kind, to help you through life."

Hawkeye began his prison term in the summer of 1996,

the same time when I had my transplant. In his first letter, written in blue ink on plain lined paper, he said, "Coach, I'm sorry for letting myself down and you because of the drugs. I'm going to make it this time, first for myself and then for you because of the love that I have for you and myself. I pray each day, Coach, that you get better for the family, me and the rest of the people who love you."

Then he said, "I know that God is working on me, Coach, and I wish I could be there for you like you have been for me all these years. I know I can't be there with you, but my prayers are there with you, Coach, because I love you and the rest of the family."

He signed it:

I love you, Coach Wootten!!
Hawkeye Whitney
Your Son!!

It is another case of touching lives without knowing it, or more than you realize. I knew I had a nice relationship with Hawkeye, but I never dreamed I had touched his life to that extent. In June I received a letter from him saying, "I wanted to send you a card for Father's Day, but they did not have any. I hope this letter will let you know how I feel about you and that I'm thinking of you on your day."

He also wrote, "I just wanted to wish you a happy Father's Day, Coach. You know you are more to me than just a coach. You are a father to me as well. So, as one of your kids, I say Happy Father's Day to you, and I pray that God will let you see many more, Coach. I'm sorry for getting this to you late, Coach, but I need to let you know how much I thank you for being a father to me!!"

He closed by saying, "Please tell the family I send them my love and prayers. And here again, Coach — Happy Father's Day to you!

Love,
Charles

Hawkeye told me last fall how thankful he was to see me doing so well after my transplant because he wants me to be around to see that he's going to make it, too. And he will. I'd bet on him.

In one of his letters during the latter stages of my recovery, he said he is convinced God spared me because He wants me to be able to point to Hawkeye as proof that you can always make it back — no matter how far you have fallen — if you put your faith in the Lord. Hawkeye has done that. And he will make it back.

He's living proof that the important thing is not that you fell down. All of us fall down from time to time. The important thing is whether you got back up. That's what Charles is doing right now in prison. He's getting back up. He's taking additional college courses. He's in a drug rehab program and has been clean for well over a year. And he has re-discovered God.

Hawkeye Whitney is standing taller all the time.

Nine

HOW TO GET TO
COLLEGE

I t was always assumed at home that we kids would be going to college after high school, but, then as now, one thing often stood in the way: money. Our mother would say to us, "Now when you're in college...," so we always had the clear understanding that we were expected to go to college. It was equally clear that we were going to have to come up with the money ourselves.

So I became a cab driver. I was "Spring 27," the identification used by the radio dispatcher of the Silver Spring Cab Company in 1952 to identify my cab. That experience strengthened my determination to go to college. I had to drive over to Baltimore, forty miles away, to get my hacker's license, what cab drivers call their "face," and as I drove through the dreadful slums along Baltimore's docks in that port town at the head of the Chesapeake Bay, all of which has since been replaced by the beautiful Harbor Place, I shook my head at the poverty and filth and said to myself, "I have to get a college education."

In December of that year, I had the pleasure of driving three of the nuns who taught me at Saint Michael's grade school in Silver Spring back to their convent on Christmas Eve. I didn't feel any embarrassment at all about being the cab driver who picked them up that night. The world needs cab drivers just as much as it needs members of other trades and professions, and the good sisters were nice enough to tell me they were proud of me for the reason I was driving that cab — to continue my education.

I did something else to get to college that parents should consider for their sons and daughters, too — I went to a two-year community college first, then moved up to the University of Maryland to complete my schooling and earn my degree in education. But whatever you and your children do to get them a college education, the most important factor of all is this: You must get started early. You can't wait until your child is starting his or her senior year in high school. That's too late. They, with your help, have to start in the ninth grade. In fact, they have to start in the first grade or even earlier by developing good study habits, working hard and establishing a good working relationship with their teachers, their counselors, their coaches if they are athletes and their parents.

Assuming this has been the case with your children and they have progressed to the best of their ability throughout their scholastic years, the questions become: What should we do and when should we do it to help our son or daughter get a good college education?

The practices we follow at DeMatha in obtaining scholarships or financial aid for our students can work for you at home, too. What follows is a description of a program you can establish with your children, whether they are athletes or not, which can be just as successful for them as the same kind of system has been for our students.

DeMatha was only ten years old when I went there in 1956, with an enrollment of only a hundred and seventy-five students. No basketball player there had ever won a scholarship. Today, four decades later, more than two hundred young men have won full, four-year scholarships to college through our program, which I established in 1960, when Johnny Herbert became our first "blue-chip" basketball star, able to take his pick of any college in the country.

DeMatha had several stars before then who attracted college interest, including Ernie Cage, Ben Spotts, Walt Coughlin and Rudy Rudelonis, but Johnny was the first one who was going to be in such a commanding position. I was in only my fourth year as DeMatha's head basketball coach and athletic director, and I was a complete novice at the business of helping to win scholarships for my players, but I felt strongly that every coach has an obligation to do everything he can to help his seniors attend the college of their choice and to win whatever kind of scholarship or financial aid might be possible for them.

Before the start of our 1960-61 season, as John Kennedy and Richard Nixon campaigned against each other and Bill Mazeroski shocked the baseball world with his home run to upset the mighty Yankees of Maris and Mantle in the World Series, I wrote a letter with a thumbnail sketch about each of our seniors, had it mimeographed and mailed it to more than three hundred college coaches.

In Johnny's case, I wrote, "Johnny Herbert is a five-foot, eight-inch, 155-pound guard, an excellent student, a great ball handler, a fine shooter and a penetrator, a winner in every respect and a good Division I prospect despite his size." I made sure to add, "He will be the valedictorian of his graduating class," which confirmed for the coaches getting the letter that Johnny was everything I was claiming. I enclosed a copy of our schedule, but not just the schedule of our games. I also enclosed copies of our schedule for pre-season scrimmages and the schedule for our daily practices.

I enthusiastically — and sincerely — invited the coaches to attend any practice, any scrimmage, any game. I went out of my way to tell them they would be welcome at DeMatha at any time, and they didn't have to make any arrangements ahead of time — all they had to do was show up. I made everything as easy as possible for the college coaches. And I did all of these things early, before the season started and before our traditional first day of practice on November 8.

It worked. We were playing Bladensburg High School, a public school in our Prince George's County, midway through our season when Johnny had one of his greatest games, scoring more than thirty points and running our floor game flawlessly. I was on my way to our locker room just after the game ended when a man walked up to me and said, "Excuse me, Coach, but I'm Coach Byron Gilbreth of Georgia Tech. I'm one of the assistants there. We got your letter, so I decided to come to your game tonight. I enjoyed watching your team play, and I particularly liked your kid, Johnny Herbert. I think we'll be interested in him."

Yes, they were. Johnny went to Tech on a full four-year scholarship, became captain of the Yellow Jackets' team, stayed in Georgia and became a highly successful real estate developer and named the main street in one of his subdivisions "Morgan Drive." He lives in Decatur, Georgia, today. Kathy and I are Godparents to his son, Steven Morgan. On the night I won the one thousandth victory of my career at DeMatha, Johnny took the trouble of driving all day from Georgia up to the Washington area to be there for the game that night.

We scored big in that first use of my brand new system.

I've made refinements over the years in what I do and how I do it, including putting together video tapes of each player with highlights of his best performances, but the system as I applied it in the case of Johnny Herbert remains fundamentally the same today and can work just as well for parents or coaches today as it did for Johnny almost forty years ago. We spell it out clearly for recruiters in writing:

DeMatha High School
Rules Regarding Recruiting

DeMatha is delighted with the great association we have with so many colleges and universities throughout the country. We feel that we have this excellent relationship due to the fact that we have always kept the lines of communication open regarding our policies on recruitment of our student athletes. With this in mind, we feel that it would be to everyone's benefit to have the rules set down in writing to avoid any misunderstandings. We want to emphasize that every college will be treated the same and that at DeMatha we never tell the players where to go to college. It is strictly their decision and theirs alone since they are the ones that will be spending four years there. To quote the old saying, "We don't tell them who to marry and we don't tell them where to go to college." With this in mind, here are the specific ground rules for college recruiters to follow:

1. All contacts must be made through the coach's office.

2. The student athlete is never called at home; nor his parents or any members of his family. (If you want them to call you, they will be delighted to call collect at their convenience.)

3. Any recruiter coming to DeMatha will have the opportunity to meet and talk with any player that he is interested in.

4. If the recruiter strikes up an interest with the young man, and the young man wants the school to visit his home, this will be set up at the convenience of both parties.

5. If the school wants the young man to visit and he wishes to visit, then we will set the visit up through the coach's office.

6. Visits are allowed throughout the fall until basketball practice starts and, of course, can resume after the season is over. Basically, we do not allow visits during the season unless there should be a legitimate gap during which time the team is not practicing.

7. If there are any questions regarding our rules, please feel free to call the coach's office.

Obviously, the effect of these rules is to make the situation fair for everyone and to remove as much pressure as possible from the student athlete's senior year. Any deviation from these rules will be an indication to us that the institution is not willing to work with the school in an honest, straightforward manner and we are confident that none of our athletes would want to play for anyone who breaks the rules.

Thank you very much for your understanding and cooperation, and I trust that this will make everything easier for the colleges, for DeMatha, and most importantly, for the student-athletes themselves.

Best wishes for every success.
Morgan Wootten
Head Basketball Coach

The keys in Johnny Herbert's case were that we provided him the right kind of guidance, and we started early. I did the same thing as recently as the week before we began writing this chapter. Kathy and I were at the annual Reebok convention in Mexico when I ran into Coach Dick Kuchen of Yale. I seized the opportunity to tell him, "We have two promising juniors who can be stars in the Ivy League and will have the academics to go to any of the schools there. They will probably be one-two in their

Photo by the Clements Family

With the Alps in the background, DeMatha's Stags enjoy the sightseeing during a trip to France in the summer of 1994. Coach Morgan Wootten and his wife, Kathy, are at the far left.

graduating class. They're great prospects for your program at Yale."

He said, "I'm going to get on that immediately."

As a result, those two juniors already are being considered by one of the most outstanding universities in America. Why? Because we started the ball rolling early.

Another essential ingredient in creating — and creating is the right word — opportunities for your seniors is to treat every coach and every college equally. Never roll out the red carpet for a big name school and then give a smaller, lesser known college the brushoff. And my strict rule against telling your kids where to go to college becomes doubly important in this process, because if the word ever got out that you were delivering seniors to certain schools, the others would stop showing up.

I also make sure to bring in each senior and show him that year's letter so the boy will see for himself exactly what we are telling the college coaches about him. We also use the letter as a communications vehicle with the student-athlete, talking the letter over with him and letting them know our evaluation of him so he will have a clear understanding of what we expect of him and what he should expect, and demand, of himself.

Those students who are not athletes have a chance to accomplish extremely helpful things for themselves, too, whether it is a full academic scholarship, financial aid or a package of small scholarships that can add up to a large percentage of their tuition and can go a long way toward paying other expenses such as books and room and board.

I have three daughters, and they all went out and got financial help through various opportunities. Our daughter Carol was a case in point. She won a scholarship of five hundred dollars from the University Park Women's Club in our community by applying and writing an essay. Cathy won a scholarship to the University of Richmond because of her academic ability and her involvement in school activities, including her work as a cheerleader. Tricia combined college with salaried jobs as she earned her degree.

The manager of our basketball team for the 1996-97 season, Chris Underwood, won a scholarship of four hundred and fifty dollars after I tipped him off about the opportunity and is now also a candidate for a Senatorial scholarship from one of Maryland's United States Senators. Chris is putting together a sizeable package of smaller scholarships that will enable him to attend the University of Maryland because he will cut his tuition in half with these scholarships.

There is a considerable amount of such scholarships and financial assistance out there for students who qualify either academically or on the basis of demonstrated need. It continues to amaze me, even though I deal in this field every day of my life, just how many of these financial resources go unknown and therefore unsolicited and un-tapped.

In fact, there are so many that some people even make a living out of offering to provide certain information services to high school students and their parents, but on this point you have to be wary. Take what they promise you with a healthy skepticism. Some of these people may be legitimate and may indeed provide you with information that can help your son or daughter to win a scholarship or receive some other form of assistance for college. But there are a lot of con artists working that game, too. Be careful. You are much safer — with the odds much more in your favor — if you work through your child's teacher, coach and guidance counselor.

I have always encouraged our seniors to visit college campuses on their own before and during their senior years, even if it is just to go to colleges and universities in your community. These visits, which students can make locally when they are sophomores and juniors in high school, give them a feel for what it's like on a college campus and will put them in a much better position to make that final decision.

I have always been a strong believer in introducing high school students to as much of the world outside their own orbit as you possibly can, and this is another valuable service which can be provided by parents. It shocks people when I tell them I have even taken our basketball team inside a state prison — the Maryland House of Corrections at Jessups — to play a game and present a clinic for the prisoners just so our student-athletes can see and hear and touch part of the world beyond high school.

College campuses are another new world to them. Driving a cab certainly contributed to my education. In later years, I found out that Al McGuire feels the same way about cab drivers. He said no one's education is truly complete until you have driven a cab for six months and been a bartender that long, too. He has a point. Nor should parents insist that their children go to college if the kids would rather become members of a trade or enter some other kind of work. That's where Harry Truman's advice to parents comes into play. If what they want to do after high school is honorable work and it's their strong desire, encourage them to do it and even help them along the way in whatever manner you can. The world needs cab drivers and even bartenders, not to mention computer technicians, plumbers, steamfitters, mechanics and airline pilots, none of which requires a college degree.

I considered that trip to the prison a valuable part of their high school education for the members of that team. I know at least one player who agreed with me. On our way back to DeMatha, he told me, "Coach, you've really done it to me this time. I don't want to hear that metal gate clang shut any more." I plan to do the same thing in the near future with our team by taking them to a kitchen for the homeless, like the Washington organization known as S.O.M.E — So Others May Eat. At S.O.M.E. our players could take their places on the serving line and serve food to homeless people. It would be another valuable addition to their education beyond the classroom walls.

Academic preparation is at least as important as putting together a financial plan for college. In the case of high school athletes, they must go through "clearing houses" established each year by the NCAA to guarantee that the student-athlete is qualified for college admission. The athletes now need at least a 2.0 grade point average in thirteen core courses in mathematics, science, languages and history, plus an acceptable SAT score determined in part by their GPA. The lower the athlete's GPA is, the higher his SAT score must be.

This is another critical reason for starting your son or daughter early, in the ninth grade, on a track that will lead them to academic success by the time they are seniors and considering their college choices. If their scores in any of those thirteen core courses are no higher than C, they need to have time to go to summer school or take some other corrective action that will raise those C's to B's or A's so their grade point average will rise accordingly. I have encouraged many of my students who received C's in these courses to go to summer school so they won't be disappointed as seniors by being told they do not qualify academically for the college of their choice.

At DeMatha, we are lucky to have my old friend, Buck Offutt, the one who gave me such eye-opening advice when I was considering that offer from North Carolina State in 1980. Buck's reputation as the best SAT tutor in the nation has helped more DeMatha students than anyone could ever count, and not just DeMatha students. There are stars in the NBA and the NFL today who still send Buck tickets to their games because they are so grateful to him for helping them get into the college they wanted to attend. The president of one of the most famous universities in the country sent his son to Washington to spend ten days under Buck's tutelage so he could get the highest score possible on his SAT exam. The vice president of one of America's best known corporations sent his daughter to Washington so Buck could spend a weekend preparing her for her SATs. Our daughter, Tricia, wanted to maximize her SAT score, so she asked Buck to help her. He raised her score two hundred points on her practice tests.

Only one school has a Buck Offutt, but all of them could have two other academic programs that DeMatha and other schools have begun in recent years: counseling for college and summer camps — not for basketball or baseball or football but for courses.

Brendan J. McGrail joined the DeMatha staff recently as its Director of College Counseling after serving as Assistant Director of Admissions at Holy Cross College in Worcester, Massachusetts. DeMatha, and only a few other schools, most of them private, have such positions in the Washington area. The program is even more rare in public schools.

Because of the awareness that students and their parents have to start the college data-gathering process well before their senior years in high school, Brendan meets with the students in the winter of their junior year and begins a series of activities to help them determine the college of their choice and to make sure they have time to prepare themselves academically so they will not be disappointed by being rejected when they apply.

He and others take DeMatha's juniors in March to a college fair conducted by the Archdiocese of Washington at Good Counsel High School in the county next to ours, where two hundred and fifty colleges have representatives on hand to provide information and literature about their schools. They prepare the students ahead of time by briefing them on what information to look for and what questions to ask about the colleges they want to learn about. They come away from the college fair with answers to their questions from their face-to-face meetings with the college representatives and in brochures and other printed material.

In April, Brendan runs a college admissions night for the parents of all DeMatha juniors. Admissions officers and financial aid officers from local colleges and universities speak, and Brendan does, too. He tells the parents that he would like to sit down with each of them and their sons before the summer begins and lay out what they should be doing next. At that meeting, he reviews what the junior has done at DeMatha in his first three years there, with Brendan looking at the student's transcript the way a college admissions officer would.

Then he does something similar to what I do with our basketball players, making a list of five college characteristics for the student's use in considering where he wants to go to college:

1. **Location** — Does the student want to go to college in the Washington area, or does he want to go away from home? If he wants to go away, how far? The Northeast? The Southwest? The Midwest? Anywhere? This decision alone narrows the hunt considerably and gets the student off to a fast start in choosing his college.

2. **Size** — Does the junior want to go to a small school, with an enrollment under three thousand students? Medium size, between three and eight thousand? Or a large university, with more than eight thousand students on campus?

3. **Campus setting** — Are they interested in an urban school located in the heart of a big city? A suburban school? Something more rural?

4. **Academic interests** — Does the student have a specific major in mind, or a curriculum he wants

Brendan Wootten swishes the winning foul shots in the 1988 city championship game.

to pursue?

5. **Extracurricular Interests** — Does the junior want
   to become active in sports or music or acting?

Brendan then takes the information he obtains from these five college characteristics and combines it with the student's grade point average, cumulative grades, SAT score and class standing. Then Brendan moves to a new step which he originated himself. From the information provided by the student in response to the five characteristics mentioned above, and still working with the student and his parents, Brendan is able to compile a preliminary list of twenty-five to thirty schools that they look into over the summer.

Many families take advantage of that summer before the senior year to visit some of the schools on Brendan's list and to obtain more information from their libraries or even on the Internet. That's the ideal time to do those things, because with the beginning of the senior year in September, the student has much less spare time and flexibility in his schedule.

When our students return in September, most of the seniors have narrowed Brendan's list down to somewhere under ten schools. Brendan says the typical DeMatha student will then apply to between four and seven colleges. For their own protection so they won't find themselves out in the cold without a college to attend, Brendan stresses that they use a "three-tier system," applying to schools where they might be a long shot because the schools are so difficult to be admitted to, to other schools on a second tier where they have about a fifty-fifty chance of being admitted, and to a third tier of schools where they can be sure they will be accepted.

Every application to college from every DeMatha senior comes across Brendan's desk — fifteen hundred every year because some students apply to as many as eight or nine colleges each. With this review, Brendan can examine every application before it is submitted to make certain it is completely accurate and represents the student's interests in the very best way.

Brendan also follows up with telephone calls to the colleges to provide any supplemental information that might be preferred and to see that the student receives his response within a reasonable period of time.

We also work with our athletes who might be candidates for athletic scholarships to make sure they meet the school's academic requirements and also as protection against the possibility of injury in their senior year. There are many cases of athletes who suffered injuries as seniors and had their athletic scholarships "pulled" by the college. However, if they are able to meet the academic standards, they can at least be admitted to the school of their choice and maybe even with an academic scholarship or some other form of financial aid.

Tim Strachan, our star quarterback, is an example. He

had offers of football scholarships from Joe Paterno at Penn State and Mark Duffner of the University of Maryland. In the summer before his senior year, while enjoying an afternoon at the beach with his family and his girlfriend, Tim suffered a broken neck when he dived into the Atlantic Ocean off Ocean City, Maryland. That didn't make any difference to Penn State or Maryland. Coaches Paterno and Duffner assured him that his scholarship was still good.

We had another case at DeMatha in which a student who was the catcher on our baseball team and also played on our hockey team, Sean Gildea, broke his foot in his last hockey game of his senior year. He was forced to miss virtually his whole senior year of baseball, but because of his strong performance in the classroom over all four of his years in high school, he was able to qualify for an academic scholarship to Mount Saint Mary's.

The help from our school to our seniors does not end there. Over the winter months, specifically in December and January, Brendan turns his time and attention to helping the seniors obtain information on the many sources of financial aid and the criteria to be met. He tells them about the four primary sources of aid — federal, state, institutional and private — based on either financial need or academic merit. He develops information for them on what they can qualify for and how to go about applying. He has been phenomenally successful in helping our graduates to obtain financial aid for their college educations. The members of our last graduating class received more than seven million dollars in assistance, thanks in great measure to Brendan's outstanding work.

Seniors usually hear from their colleges in February and March and have until May 1 to submit their deposits. By that time, Brendan has already begun to work with the next class of juniors.

Three members of the DeMatha faculty are helping to break new ground in preparing students to perform better academically so they can have a more successful high school career and thus enhance their prospects for college.

Dr. Dan McMahon, the chairman of the English department; Pat Smith, the department's co-chairman, and Tom Krawczewicz, the head of our journalism department, conducted a summer class — called "The Write Place" — for twenty-one students in the summer of 1997, not to teach them basketball or any other sport but to assist them in improving their writing skills so they can perform better in all subjects. They are following the lead of Rick Reeves, chairman of DeMatha's science department, who started a week-long day camp two summers earlier for students interested in studying more about science and the environment.

The English students made field trips to *The Washington Post*, to a wildlife refuge in Patuxent, Maryland, the new journalism museum in the Virginia suburbs and even a matinee movie. The students are required to write reports on their field trips to show not only their writing ability but also their powers of observation, including their interpretations of what they saw. They also are given exercises in analytical thinking.

After the trip to the wildlife preserve, for example, the students had to write a description of what they saw as an exercise in descriptive writing. Then the group discussed the writings of Emerson and Thoreau in describing their surroundings in New England. After the trip to the "Newseum," their assignment was to write a composition on the difference between news and editorial writing. After the movie, they had to write a review, like a critic. They get to do all their writing on the school's computers and use our software programs for "spell-checking" and other tools and techniques of writing in the 1990s.

While they were at *The Post*, two students happened to come into a bonus. A local television reporter, Tom Sherwood, a former *Post* reporter and now seen on Station WRC-TV, the Washington NBC station, was taping a feature story on the twenty-fifth anniversary of the Watergate break-in. Two of the students were interviewed and got to see themselves on the evening news.

Most of the students were boys entering the ninth grade at DeMatha, but some were entering the seventh and eighth grades at other schools. All of them were welcome, and all attended on a voluntary basis. They were allowed to come casual instead of the usual DeMatha dress code of coat and tie. They were allowed to wear shorts, but they were required to maintain a neat, clean appearance.

The project took a full week out of their summer, with each day's class lasting from 8:30 to 3:30. Most of them stayed later every day to talk to their teachers and fellow students. The school is not able to give them academic credit for their week's work, but the response from parents and students alike was so enthusiastic that people at DeMatha hope to expand the program to other subjects as well as to students in other grades.

Ten
THE REST OF YOUR PACKAGE

I n recent years, colleges and universities have been placing greater emphasis all the time on a high school student's extra-curricular activities. Students do not have to be athletes to show they are involved in school activities. In fact, schools want to see that even athletes are doing other things as part of their involvement in school life besides just playing ball.

Parents should encourage their students when they enter the ninth grade to become involved in other activities — the newspaper, the yearbook, the chess club, the Spanish or 4-H clubs or any other club, intramural sports, student government, the band, running for class office. All of those activities are integral parts of school life, and the colleges that your children are interested in attending will want to see some evidence that they were involved in school and were not the old 9-to-3-then-go-home student of previous generations.

I have told many parents, including myself, that helping your child to choose the right college in any way you can — by providing advice, money or just by listening to their ideas and questions — is the last great thing you will be able to do for them as their parent. I believe that with all my heart, and that belief sustained Kathy and me as we tried to meet our responsibilities toward all five of our children in those pivotal years of their lives.

That same advice came back to haunt me in the case of our son, Brendan, and the culprit was Bob Ferry. When Bob Jr. was selecting a college, he was leaning strongly toward Harvard, which was his eventual selection. But Harvard is an Ivy League school, and those schools are prohibited from awarding athletic scholarships. Instead, they give financial assistance, but that is based on demonstrated need.

Bob Sr., as the general manager of the Washington Bullets, couldn't make any case at all that he and his family were living below the poverty line, so he was looking at the reality of the situation: One hundred thousand dollars over the next four years for his son's college education if he went to Harvard, or nothing if he chose any of the other schools who were actively recruiting him.

McDonald's Photo

Coach Wootten shows players and coaches in Taiwan his way to succeed, at his special clinic sponsored by McDonald's Restaurants in 1988.

He was talking to me about his six-figure dilemma when I turned philosopher and told him, "Bob, remember, this is the last great thing you'll be able to do for Bobby. You should be willing to do it. In fact, you should be proud to. You shouldn't even hesitate."

He agreed, Bob Jr. went to Harvard, and Bob Sr. was out a hundred thousand dollars over the following four years.

Now fast-forward to our son Brendan's senior year of high school. He has some scholarship offers, too, but he wants to go to the University of Pennsylvania, another Ivy League school and thus bound by the same restrictions. I was faced with the same prospect Bob Ferry had been confronted with only a few years before. That's when I found out Ferry's memory is as good as his sense of humor.

He called me and repeated my comments to him so accurately you would have thought he had recorded them when we were talking about Bob Jr.'s desire to go to Harvard. He told me, "Remember, Morgan, this is the last great thing you'll be able to do for Brendan. You should be willing to do it. In fact, you should be proud to. You shouldn't even hesitate."

So Brendan went to Penn, and I was out as much money as Bob had been. What goes around...

Coaches must be willing to devote a certain amount of their time to helping their seniors obtain scholarships or at least to get into the college of their choice. I spend up to twenty percent of my time during the basketball season working on this part of my responsibilities.

In one case, I spent well over a year helping one of our players to get a scholarship by convincing a college coach that his value would go beyond his playing skills. I told the coach at the school the boy had targeted, "This kid is a winner. You'd be getting the total package if you offer him a scholarship. He's not a great shooter, but he's a hard-knocking player." Then it occurred to me to ask, "How good is your academic support system?"

He answered, "Pretty good. It should be better in terms of our tutoring and that type of thing, but it's pretty good."

I said, "If you take this kid, you'll be getting a built-in tutor. This kid would make a great tutor for your players. He can tutor anybody. You'll never have a player ineligible on your basketball team. He's that good. And you know yourself that your players would rather be tutored by a fellow player than by a teacher."

The coach agreed, and the kid got his scholarship. Sure enough, he became a great tutor, but he also became something more than that — a member of Phi Betta Kappa as a junior. He also had a successful career as a college basketball player. Today he is a successful professional in a large Eastern city.

Athletes and non-athletes can adjust their plans accordingly as their situations and preferences change during their high school years. We had three seniors on our 1996-97 team who decided that they would set their sights on going to a Division III school and playing more instead of trying to make it at the much tougher Division I level. Division III schools are prohibited by the NCAA from offering athletic scholarships, so I helped all three to put financial packages together.

Because of our letter to coaches every Fall about our seniors, coaches from Division III schools knew these three seniors were interested in their level of competition, so they were willing to come to our games and evaluate those three. I'm sure the thought occurred to them, "Hey — we could get a DeMatha player." It worked out, and all three of those boys are now happily on their way to receiving a solid education and enjoying themselves as college athletes.

Coaches and parents can work together to win financial aid for non-athletes such as managers of the school's sports teams. One of our basketball managers, Jeff Hathaway, is just such a success story.

Jeff came to me as a freshman and said he wanted to become a manager. I encouraged him to try out for the job of manager for the freshman team, but he wouldn't hear of that. He wanted to be the varsity manager, even though he was only in the ninth grade. To my amazement,

Morgan Wootten holds the basketball commemorating his 900th coaching victory at DeMatha during ceremonies two days later dedicating the school's gymnasium in his name. From left, his former blue-chip star, Ernie Cage; Morgan's son, Joe Wootten; Morgan's wife, Kathy, and former DeMatha Basketball Manager Jeff Hathaway, now the Associate Athletic Director at the University of Conneticut. At the dedication, Father James Day, then the rector of DeMatha, said, "Morgan, we are naming this gym after you not because you've won 900 games but for the lives you have touched, the futures you have shaped, and the Christian life you have lived."

he was good enough to handle the job and became the manager for our varsity basketball team for all four of his years at DeMatha. By his senior year, he was my righthand man in various capacities and not just in matters dealing with being a manager. He was more like an assistant athletic director.

Managers have to be willing to work hard without getting any of the glory that the players get, they have to be loyal, they have to be able to get along with people even during stressful situations and they have to possess an instinct for anticipating crises and opportunities before they arise.

Jeff was and is that kind of a young man. Today he is the highly respected Associate Athletic Director at the University of Connecticut.

John Stoddard is another example, a manager who won a scholarship, to Villanova. Chris Bates, who handled the manager's responsibilities in the 1980s, won a full scholarship to the University of Charleston. The university's coaches spotted Chris and his good work during their trips to scout our players.

Parents and coaches should always remember that to qualify for any kind of financial aid the student's academic record must first be good enough to get him or her into the school. Everything comes back to that. That's where goals come in. And something we do in our basketball program can be used by parents at home with their children, athletes or not.

As part of helping our players to maximize their college prospects, I have every player fill out a form at the beginning of each school year. I keep a copy, and I give him one.

The form asks such questions as:

- ◆ What did you do to improve yourself as a basketball player during the summer just ended?
- ◆ What areas did you improve in the most?
- ◆ What are your greatest strengths?
- ◆ What are your weaknesses?
- ◆ What are you going to do between now and November 8 to improve your weaknesses?

On the back of the form, I have the player write down his academic goals for the new school year, then his basketball goals and a description of how he intends to achieve both sets of goals. That's what parents can do at home — have their kids write down their goals for the coming school year. Making them write them down is a critical part of the effectiveness of this technique, because by putting their goals in writing, the students are making a promise to themselves.

Another important and helpful step is to take out that list of goals from time to time and go over them with your son or daughter and evaluate their progress toward those goals. You can break them out in November or so and say,

"Well, Mary — you said one of your goals at school this year would be to study at least two hours every school night and make the honor roll. Well, you're not studying two hours a night. You just got your first report card, and you didn't make the honor roll. Let's discuss your goals for a while."

By the same token, you can break out that list and discover that your child is exceeding the goals, which is a great time for a pat on the back and for the comment that our kids need to hear from us from time to time — that we're proud of them.

That's an essential part of helping your kids to make it in life — telling them you love them and are proud of them. Maybe they know it anyhow, but all of us need to hear it — at any age — and especially young people. They've earned our love and our pride, but they need to hear it — from us.

Setting goals is essential for anyone's success in life. And making a list of their goals in what becomes a contract with themselves provides the motivation that leads to success.

Eleven

The journey along a road of curves and hills that led me to that bed in Johns Hopkins University Hospital began, without my knowledge, in the spring of 1952, just before I turned twenty-one, when there was an outbreak of hepatitis at Saint Joseph's Home. Many of the orphans caught the disease, and so did a few of the staff, including me. Under doctor's orders, I spent the next six weeks in bed at the National Naval Medical Center in Bethesda, Maryland, where the presidents go for their checkups and medical treatment and where President Clinton underwent his knee surgery in 1997.

Actually, my bed rest wasn't six weeks. It was only five

185

weeks and six and a half days. I slipped out of the hospital one afternoon to coach our orphans' basketball team in the final game for the CYO championship at Catholic University. We lost, but those orphans were ecstatic just to be playing in that game. They had never experienced the thrill of playing for a basketball championship. Then I slipped back into the hospital and slid back under the covers. Nobody ever missed me.

After my recovery but before my release, the Navy doctors checked my liver to make sure it had not been damaged by the hepatitis. They said it was fine. Five years later, I underwent an appendectomy. They checked my liver again. It was still fine.

After I started getting annual physicals in 1971 with my family physician, Dr. Stan Silverberg, the report was always the same — elevated levels, indicating infection or irritation, but nothing to worry about. Not yet, anyhow.

Meanwhile, the doctors tried everything to get those levels down closer to the normal range. Nothing made a difference, so they decided just to continue monitoring the liver and checking it carefully each year during my physical exams.

The readings began to increase in 1991, indicating more irritation. That's when Dr. O'Kieffe suspected the PBC. He told me its cause is unknown. It is rarely found in men. It's not infectious. It's not from drinking. One thing they do know is that it is sometimes familial — it runs in the family. But nobody in my family has ever had a liver problem. Who knows? The only explanation I have been able to come up with before or since is it might have come from that attack of hepatitis. In 1994 I had a liver biopsy, which confirmed the PBC. Dr. O'Kieffe put me on a special drug to slow down the process. He said I may live forever, but if the PBC continued to progress a transplant would be the only solution.

At the end of the 1995-96 basketball season, Kathy and I went to Deep Creek Lake in the Allegheny Mountains of Western Maryland for a long weekend. After a brisk hike in the woods, I woke up the next morning with a swollen stomach. The doctors saw it was an umbilical hernia. Dr. Frank Sanzaro, chief of surgery at Providence Hospital in Washington, took another look, just in case, and saw more. "We have problems. Big problems. It's also the liver."

My stomach was filling up with fluid. So were my ankles. Dr. O'Kieffe put me on diuretics to reduce the fluid but warned me that I would now have to face that option he first mentioned years before — a liver transplant.

It was time to tell the kids. I did it one-on-one. I told each of them I'd had this liver problem, it was getting worse and I would need a transplant. But I sugar-coated it as much as I could, while being careful not to deceive them. I told them transplants were becoming routine, and it didn't seem to be anything to worry about.

Morgan Wootten celebrates his 900th coaching victory at DeMatha with wife Kathy (on Morgan's right) and family and friends in 1989.

The day after I told our daughter Cathy, the family's designated worrier, she said, "Hey, wait a minute! You're talking about a transplant! This is serious!" We've told that story many times since, and it's always good for a laugh — now.

It was the start of the second week of my 1996 summer basketball camp at Mount Saint Mary's, a college of gray stone buildings and rambling open green fields just off Route 15 near Emmitsburg, Maryland. I remember finishing lunch in the cafeteria and telling our camp staff, "All right, fellas — see you downstairs in about ten minutes for orientation."

I was feeling fine but tired, which didn't surprise me. I had been feeling that way much of the time in the past year. In the previous three weeks, the fatigue seemed worse, but nothing to get alarmed about.

I headed across the lobby to the office. As I walked alone, I thought to myself, "Boy, I feel terrible." There were no chairs in the lobby, but I felt I just had to sit down somewhere, anywhere. I detoured toward the men's room a few steps ahead. My intention was simply to sit on the toilet lid and rest for a minute because the toilet was the closest thing resembling a chair.

That men's room is not a busy one. When I opened the door, the room was empty. That's the last thing I remember for the next ten days. And that's when the two camp counselors spotted me collapsing.

"Dad Has Fainted"

As Joe was speeding with me in the ambulance to the Gettysburg Hospital, my daughter, Carol, who is also on our camp staff, called home to Kathy. "Dad has fainted," she said, making sure to add that the emergency medical technicians thought it was dehydration and exhaustion. Kathy, with her nurse's training and experience, agreed, especially since she knew I was on diuretics. She calmly threw a few things together in case she decided to stay overnight in Gettysburg, grabbed a quick something to eat, climbed into our other car and drove, by herself, up Routes 270 and 15 to Gettysburg Hospital, two hours away, just across the Mason-Dixon Line.

Kathy has told me since that the only time she became anxious during her drive was when she got to Gettysburg. The summer tourists on that Sunday afternoon were clogging the streets and Kathy became concerned about how much longer it might take her to get to the hospital. She thought to herself, "I'm up here already, but now I can't get to the hospital. Get out of the way, people!" But she didn't say anything. She just kept plodding her way through that last mile or two.

While her frustrations grew, Joe and Carol were talking to me, trying to keep me from lapsing into unconsciousness, even quoting Churchill back to me. I was losing eleven pints of blood. Then, they remember, I seemed to go limp, and, as Joe says, "Every buzzer in the hospital went off, and twelve people raced into the room and told us to get out."

Joe says he thinks I "flatlined" at that point, where the instruments whose lines have been going up and down to indicate the activity of various organs suddenly went straight — flat.

To make matters even more hectic for everyone involved, there was a reenactment that day of the battle of Gettysburg in the Civil War, and some of the Union and Confederate troops injured themselves. Joe and Carol said troops were showing up with sprains and cuts and other minor injuries, adding to the workload in the already high-pressure atmosphere of the emergency room.

Just after that, Kathy finally reached the hospital in the middle of Gettysburg. She was met by Joe and Carol, who took her immediately into a cubicle — she still remembers it was the second one on the right — just off the emergency room, sealed off with a curtain around my bed for privacy. She says she took one look at me and knew how "terribly serious" it was. With her nurse's training and her first-hand knowledge of my own case, she knew one other thing, too: Somehow, somebody had to get me to Baltimore, to Johns Hopkins University Hospital, as soon as possible.

One of the first questions facing her when she arrived involved the news media. Somehow, the word had been flashed by someone at our camp back to Washington that I was in a hospital in Gettysburg. The reporters had already started calling, seven of them just in the first half-hour after I was carried in there.

A nurse asked Kathy whether a well-known Washington sports reporter was really Morgan's cousin. He isn't. After that episode, the medical staff handled the media until experienced help arrived. Our camp's codirector and my long-time friend, Jim Phelan, has 45 years of experience as a college head coach — he's the basketball coach at Mount Saint Mary's — so he stepped in and handled media relations. He told Kathy, "You take care of Morgan, and I'll take care of the media."

Carol spotted a man in the emergency room who might have been a reporter. He was dressed in casual summer clothes, including a striped sports shirt, not looking at all like the professional medical people in the room, so she went right at him. She was going to throw him out of there, and she wasn't going to allow any more media people in there.

She went over to him and challenged him, demanding to know, "Who are you?"

The man Carol had spotted as a reporter answered, "I'm Dr. So-and-so. And who are you?"

The increased media watch would take care of the future, but the word was already flashing around the Washington and Baltimore news media. The story was on the TV news that Sunday night and in the papers the next morning, including an article in the *Baltimore Sun* under a headline that said it all:

DeMATHA'S WOOTTEN IN CRITICAL CONDITION
Legendary Coach Passed Out at Camp

While Joe and Carol alerted family members, Kathy tried to reach Dr. O'Kieffe back home and Dr. Vinod Rustgi at Fairfax County Hospital in the Virginia suburbs of Washington. I had been on the waiting list for a liver since April at Hopkins and Fairfax, in category three, when the patient is still able to lead a normal life. Fairfax gave me a pager, one of those beepers, for use in an emergency, but they said I wouldn't need it yet. Both hospitals estimated in April that I was close to a year away from needing a transplant. I collapsed three months later.

I had passed all the tests to insure that I was otherwise healthy and could withstand the rigors of eight hours of surgery. They threw everything at me — CT scan, MRI, stress test. Every organ in my body was tested, even a "dental write-off" to make sure my gums were healthy enough not to bleed during surgery.

The organ donor people take every precaution they can think of to make sure you have a good chance of benefiting from the organ transplant. Otherwise, they feel they might waste an organ on a patient who might die soon from another cause, instead of giving it to someone who could live for a number of years.

For example, the doctors never would have given that

transplant to Mickey Mantle a year before my illness if they had found out before the surgery, instead of after, that he had cancer. The theory in those cases is that you are wasting a good organ on a patient who was already dying from another cause.

Drs. O'Kieffe and Rustgi were both unavailable, but Kathy, after a series of frantic calls, was finally able to locate their partners. She just happened to be on the phone talking to Dr. Rustgi's associate when one of the doctors who had been working on me came out of my cubicle. Kathy says she spotted him and quickly handed the phone to him and said, "Here — you talk to him."

The two doctors, one familiar with my history and the other working on me that day, were able to exchange thoughts and recommendations on what had to be done, and how and when, to stabilize me so I could be airlifted to Hopkins or Fairfax.

At the same time, Kathy had people calling around Gettysburg trying to find a priest who could hurry to the hospital and give me the last rites of the Catholic church for people in critical condition.

The priest arrived and began giving me the Sacrament. At that same time, Tricia also arrived. She says today that she felt a "spiritual presence" when she looked at the priest, as if a Higher Being were telling her that there would be some tough times ahead, but everything was going to work out. She says today that my month in the hospital wasn't nearly as trying on her as it was for the rest of the family, because of the assurance she felt emanating from the priest that I was going to make it.

Tricia's experience helped me as much as it did her, because she was a tremendous help throughout my month in the hospital. She was almost an assistant nurse in what she did and how much assistance she provided. As she says now, she sort of grew up in hospitals because she has had epilepsy since infancy and has been in hospitals often enough that the environment almost feels natural to her. She is not intimidated by the hospital scene and feels that her epilepsy has made her a stronger person. All of that worked to both her advantage and mine during my month at John Hopkins.

After several hours of drama and feverish work, the doctors and their nurses were able to stabilize me. Now I could be flown by helicopter to Baltimore, right to the landing pad at Johns Hopkins, which was closer, among other reasons, than Fairfax. Kathy remembers that my condition was so precarious they used an ambulance to get me from the hospital to the chopper, which was waiting only a hundred feet or so away.

No member of our family was allowed on the helicopter, so they drove their own cars to Baltimore. When they arrived at the hospital, they were greeted by a surprising sight — our son, Brendan, was waiting there with his fiance, Elizabeth. My sister, Lee, was also there.

Brendan and Elizabeth had been out enjoying the splendid mild summer afternoon when one of our family members reached him through the pager he uses in connection with his work as a stock broker. He and Elizabeth jumped into Brendan's car and headed straight for Baltimore and beat everybody who drove only from Gettysburg and Washington.

What was so incredible about that? Brendan and Elizabeth were in New York. He still denies that he is wanted in four states for speeding.

On arrival at Hopkins, I was immediately leap-frogged over category two and became a category one candidate — death is imminent without a transplant almost immediately. As a long-time history teacher, I have since thought about the story Abraham Lincoln told about the convicted criminal who was sentenced to be run out of town on the rail.

When one of the townspeople asked him how he felt about it, Lincoln said the criminal answered, "If it wasn't for the honor of the thing, I'd just as soon walk."

In looking back, I think that might have been my feeling if I had been conscious — if it weren't for the honor of being number one, I would have preferred not to be facing the frightening future which loomed right in front of me.

When that first liver arrived and then proved unsuitable, Kathy says it was a jolting reminder to her that this whole thing was far from automatic, that maybe they transplant a lot of organs these days, but the odds might still be stacked against you in any given case. Mine might turn out to be one of them. Nine people in this country die every day waiting for an organ.

That happened to another patient on my floor. The right organ never came along. The patient simply ran out of time and died while waiting for an organ that never arrived.

Kathy and the rest of the family, except Brendan and Joe who maintained an all-night vigil at the hospital, were resting at a nearby motel when she received a phone call from the hospital at 5:30 A.M. on Wednesday, the start of my third full day at Johns Hopkins. A second, healthier liver had arrived. The doctors were going to perform the transplant surgery.

The family members rushed from the motel to the hospital, said some prayers at my bedside and kissed me — while I slept through it all — just before the staff wheeled me out of the room and toward the operating room. At about 9:15, the receptionist in their waiting room told them a phone call had just come down from the O.R. to tell the family the surgery had just begun. Two hours later, another call came down informing the family that things were going well and the doctors were happy.

Then Father Damian Anuszewski of DeMatha, who had also given me the last rites, arrived from Hyattsville and said Mass for my family at the old Baltimore Basilica nearby. Knowing that the entire procedure could take between twelve and eighteen hours, the family went to lunch after Mass, with Kathy reminding herself, "This is going to be a long, long day." They returned to the hospital at 1:15. To their utter shock and delight, there was a message waiting for them: "The liver is in and functioning."

Kathy says Dr. Thuluvath came into the waiting room at 2:15, and he had a faint smile on his face. Her reaction to herself was, "Oh boy!" She says today, "I knew he had good news. His body language was so good." He gave the family the encouraging report that everything was going smoothly and my doctors were optimistic. At 2:45, Dr. Burdick came out of surgery and told the family the transplant had gone well and briefed them on what they could expect over the next several days. The family was allowed to visit me for a few minutes that evening. Kathy says the improvement in my condition was immediately noticeable, even though I was unconscious, because of my improved color. The jaundiced appearance was gone. She says she leaned over and kissed me on my cheek.

Dr. Burdick, my surgeon, said later he considered me an example of someone who was on the brink of death and yet came back quickly. He said that even after more than ten years in the liver transplantation field, he is still surprised that "the patient can get so much better so fast, because the liver is so central to the rest of the body's problems."

In discussing my case, Dr. Burdick said, "In the space of only a few days, he went from being critically, deathly ill to recovering nicely. It's still one of the amazing features of liver transplantation. The biology of it is really quite striking to me."

He also said success stories like mine come with a secondary message to the professionals in the field. "We have to remind ourselves," he said, "of the limits to our capacities. Not every patient is going to do this well. When we get somebody like this, we have to remind ourselves not to get too inflated."

Twelve

During my thirty-two days at Johns Hopkins, we were deluged by mail and gifts both there and at our home back in Hyattsville. It was a continuing avalanche of more than three thousand cards, letters and telegrams, over a hundred boxes of candy and baskets of fruit, more than a hundred floral arrangements, and phone calls from all over, even from the governor, Parris Glendening — twice.

While I was in intensive care in the first days after the transplant, still unconscious, the family established a code word to screen all the phone calls. They decided on "Valerie," Kathy's first name, which she never uses. If the caller didn't know the code, the call was not put through.

I was struck repeatedly by the genuine thoughtfulness of people. The most impressive example of all came from Kathy. After I was moved from the intensive care unit to interim care and then into my own room, she set up a cot and slept in the same room. She didn't go home for three weeks, until I was discharged.

The letters were the most inspiring to me. They came from people you would hope to hear from — family members, my DeMatha colleagues, long-time friends. But they came from others, too —my former players, their parents, my coaching rivals, members of the news media, local and state officials.

Some of the messages that inspired me the most were from people I don't know, who just felt moved to write to me. They were the ones who began their letters by saying, "You don't know me, Coach, but…"

Like the staff member at the National Institutes of Health who referees high school and college basketball games in his spare time. He sent me a three-page, single-spaced letter and told me, "Like yourself, I suffer from liver disease, chronic hepatitis B …With all your great accomplishments in the game of basketball, nothing compares with your leadership in the game of life. You have taught us how to live with integrity and never give up."

The sister of a 45-year-old middle management executive who had just been laid off because his company is "down-sizing" wrote to thank me for snapping him out of his worries.

"Coach," his sister wrote, "I hope you know what an inspiration you are to all who are touched by you. Your record is phenomenal, but that is really secondary to the integrity, courage, commitment and responsibility you demonstrate in your daily activities and life. You are a model for all people, and you have given my brother hope and inspiration in a way that nobody else could. I thank you for that."

I heard from a woman I don't know who is a business consultant in Brazil. A Washington lawyer wrote a nice note, as did a high school coach in Indiana, a man in prison, a middle school science teacher, a girls' basketball coach in Winnipeg, Canada, and literally many hundreds more.

College coaches I've worked with at clinics and shared the speaker's platform with at functions all over the country sent me heartwarming notes. Denny Crum of the University of Louisville said, "Our game is better because of the impact you have had on players and coaches from coast to coast." John Wooden, UCLA's Hall of Fame coach, was another who wrote, plus Dale Brown of Louisiana State, Dean Smith of North Carolina, Duke's Mike Krzyzewski and Bobby Cremins of Georgia Tech, who said, "You have always inspired me, and I'll never forget your talking to me when I was just a graduate assistant."

The Value of a Greeting Card

My friend and colleague of forty years, Red Auerbach, stayed in close touch. He's the one who sent me his own kind of sentimental message almost twenty years before, in 1978, when we won the sixth hundredth victory of my coaching career. Red was still the president of the Boston Celtics then, and he sent me a note on Celtics letterhead saying —

> Dear Morgan:
> I just picked up the *Basketball Weekly* and saw your ugly face six times.

Then he congratulated me. This time around, he played it straight.

Football coaches wrote too, including Bobby Ross, who was then still coaching the San Diego Chargers and is now the head coach of the Detroit Lions, and Penn State's Joe Paterno, who was kind enough to say, "Take care of yourself — a lot of people need you."

The executive director of the International Association of Approved Basketball Officials wrote that his organization was establishing a scholarship in my name for a Special Olympics athlete wishing to become a basketball official. He said they were doing it "to celebrate your recovery."

Imagine getting over three thousand cards and letters, with many of them saying that same kind of thing. Every member of the incoming freshman class at DeMatha, all

The three most successful basketball coaches of all time — college, pro and high school — visit at the GTE Academic Awards Hall of Fame dinner in Washington in 1994. From left, UCLA's John Wooden, the Boston Celtics' Red Auerbach and DeMatha's Morgan Wootten.

two hundred and twenty-five of them, wrote me individual letters during their summer retreat and orientation before starting their high school careers. I read every one of them, twenty or so every night.

Who wouldn't get well with that kind of support, even from strangers? Brendan strung some of the cards across the walls of my room, literally wallpapering the room.

One of the lasting lessons I learned from that whole experience: I will never underestimate the value of a greeting card. My family whispered the names of some of the senders to me in the first days after my surgery. When I grew stronger, I was able to read them for myself. Their impact is far greater than I ever could have imagined, because you are struck by the utter thoughtfulness of the senders. They're not asking for a reply or anything else. They just want to take time to send you a card to let you know you are in their thoughts and prayers.

When you are as sick as I was, and even those who are not necessarily in a life-or-death situation, just to know that people are thinking about you gives you an uplifting feeling that the senders themselves can't even appreciate fully unless they have been in the same situation.

The whole ordeal, which was so exhaustive for so many people, was not without its lighter moments, beginning the minute I woke up ten days after collapsing. Under the influence of several different kinds of strong medication and still half-punchy from being unconscious for that long, I saw our daughter, Carol, in the room with me. She was wearing a big smile on her face.

I sensed that I was in a hospital setting of some kind, but I wasn't sure. In fact, I was sure of only one thing — I had to get out of there. I immediately told Carol, "Get my clothes, and let's get everything together. I'm outta here."

Carol said, "I don't think the doctors would approve."

I repeated to her "Carol, I have to get out of here."

After all, I knew I was a busy man. Then I spotted Kathy behind Carol.

"Hi, Honey," I said. "How are you doing?" Then I told her the same thing. "Get my clothes. I have to get out of here."

Kathy repeated the same response as Carol, that the doctors would never approve, which, of course, was right, but not in my foggy mind. I said, "I've already talked to the doctors. I've cleared it with them. C'mon, let's go."

Carol and Kathy both had big grins on their faces while I was trying to convince them I was right. At that moment, Dr. Ken Chavin came into the room and caught the last part of the conversation. He said, "What's the problem here, Coach?"

I said to him, "I have to get out of here. I have places to go and things to do." I didn't know where I was or why I was there. I just knew somehow that I was supposed to leave.

Dr. Chavin said, "Let's wait twenty-four to forty-eight hours. If everything looks good then, we can let you leave."

I said, "Okay. I can live with that, I guess."

It was crazy talk, but I didn't know it. I was flat on my back at the time. And I stayed that way for the next several days.

I looked around later and tried to figure out where I was. I saw a newspaper with a headline that said, "WOOTTEN NEEDS NEW LIVER OR WILL DIE." I asked Kathy, "Did they write a follow-up to this story?"

Then there was the time I became disoriented, leading to a most uncharacteristic habit of swearing at people and began to challenge my doctors. With her nurse's experience, Kathy right away suspected that the culprit might be one of the anti-rejection drugs routinely given to transplant patients. But the doctors weren't convinced, so they continued their medicine, and I continued my cursing. They did so at their own risk. I threw all of them out of my room one day. As a parting shot, I called one of them "Dr. Kervorkian."

The first great athlete I ever coached, Angelo Marini, visited me around this time. When he asked Kathy why I was cursing when I had never done it before, she told him the story. Angelo, ever the diplomat, asked one of my doctors, "Doctor, if you were on duty in an emergency room on a Saturday night and they brought in a patient who was cussing and doing things he doesn't do otherwise, what would your guess be?"

The doctor said, "I would immediately suspect drugs."

Angelo said, "Does that tell you something?"

The doctor changed my medication. The guilty drug, whatever it was, left my system within forty-eight hours, and my language was socially acceptable again.

Jack Bruen came down from our basketball camp to visit me. Jack has helped me to operate our camp for 25 years. After my collapse, while Joe was in Baltimore, Jack kept the camp running smoothly. He had me laughing so hard I was crying as he told me about Angelo, with nothing but good intentions, stepping in and showing his willingness to take charge of things at the camp on the day of my collapse.

At first, according to Jack, Angelo's thought was that Joe, my son, should take control. Jack said Angelo gripped Joe around the shoulders as they were preparing me for the ambulance ride to the Gettysburg Hospital and said, "Joe, you have to step in now and take over for your father. You've been trained for this all your life. Now you have to step up and be the man."

But Joe said, "That's my father they're putting in the ambulance. I'm not staying here. I'm going to the hospital with him."

The Value of a Greeting Card

So Angelo, recognizing a crisis when he sees one, told whoever else was around, "All right, then. That means there's only one other person up here who should take control of things, and that's me."

Jack said Angelo turned to him and said, "The first thing I have to do is to hold a meeting with all three of the commissioners." We have "commissioners" who help us to run the games and the leagues in each camp. The only problem with what Angelo was saying about a meeting with all three commissioners is that we had six commissioners.

Jack told me that Angelo then spotted a coach, grabbed him and gave him a gung-ho John Wayne-Jack Nicholson Marine motivational talk, saying, "I want you to give me the very best week of your life!"

Whereupon Jack was forced to say, "Angelo — let him go. He's a coach at the baseball camp."

The nurses thought the medicine was making me wacky. They must have been convinced I was hallucinating. In my first day or two after regaining consciousness, I was watching the Olympics on TV from Atlanta when I told the nurse who happened to be in the room at the time that I had coached two players in high school who helped the United States to win the gold medal at the 1976 Olympics. "Sure, Mr. Wootten," she said. "Sure you did."

A few days later another nurse brought me a soft drink. When I asked her what kind of a drink it was, she told me it was a Coke. I told her I would drink it but that I've always felt a certain loyalty to Pepsi because my grandmother designed the Pepsi-Cola logo. This nurse had the same kind of reaction as the first one: "Sure she did, Mr. Wootten."

I explained that my grandmother was Bayard Wootten — Bayard is my middle name — and that she was a renowned artist and photographer in the south, with studios in various Southern cities. She was born in New Bern, North Carolina, where Pepsi was established in the early years of this century. I said my grandmother used to enjoy telling anyone who would listen that Pepsi offered to pay her five hundred dollars for her work or pay her in Pepsi-Cola stock, whichever she preferred. She took the cash.

She was so prominent as a photographer, not just as an artist, that the Wright Brothers, whose first flight was in North Carolina at Kitty Hawk, hired her to take aerial photographs during one of their first flights. She was probably the first woman to fly and certainly was the first to take a photograph from an airplane in flight. With all this supporting information to document my claim about her designing the Pepsi logo, don't you know that nurse still didn't believe me?

There was a third nurse, an African-American, and we got to talking one day about the "underground railway," the network of homes and churches and other locations

Photo by Edward Potskowski

The media made a big story in 1993 out of Coach Wootten's one thousandth basketball victory.

which served as underground safe havens for slaves after they escaped from their masters and were secretly making their way north to the Canadian border during and after the Civil War.

I mentioned that my great-great-grandmother's house in Chapel Hill, North Carolina, where Dean Smith coaches the Tar Heels today, was a stop on the underground railway. Again I provided supporting information: I said that when they tore my great-great-grandmother's house down, the demolition crew found artifacts in a sub-basement documenting that slaves had hidden there on their way north.

She didn't believe me, either.

The strong spiritual support I received while in the hospital obviously was a major factor in fueling my recovery. The messages played a role there, too, and so did the hospital chaplains who brought me Communion every morning. As I continued to improve, I found myself wondering why my life had been spared. I was confident that I was going to make it all the way back to full health and my normal lifestyle, but I didn't know why.

As I lay in my hospital bed that month, I made sure to say plenty of prayers of thanksgiving. I told God I was thankful for the second life He was giving me, but I found myself asking Him, "Why was I spared? What is the reason that You kept me alive?" I thought back to my dream and wondered just why Saint Peter told me, "Go on back.

I don't need you right now." The answer didn't come in the hospital. It came later.

A month in a hospital and undergoing an organ transplant does wonders for your sense of values. People ask me now what my low points in the hospital were. I never had any. There was no real pain associated with my experience, only extreme discomfort. But you can put up with discomfort. I was even able to put up with the food. With all my medication, I had no real sense of taste. Everything I ate tasted like sawdust. But I knew I had to get that food into me if I were to regain my strength, so in effect I force-fed myself so I could get strong enough again to go home.

The only serious problem — it was more of an adjustment than a problem — developed when my muscles atrophied on me because I had been flat on my back for a month, never using any muscles. By the time I was recovering from the transplant surgery, all the muscles in my body had just wasted away because of a lack of use.

The nurses had to work with me to do such simple things as brushing my teeth. Just picking up the brush was an ordeal. Moving the brush back and forth across my teeth seemed impossible in my first few attempts. When I finally progressed to the point where I could pick up the brush and use it, brushing my teeth was a monumental chore that took ten minutes, and even then I didn't do a good job. Shaving took twenty minutes.

Three weeks after my transplant operation, I was considered ready for physical therapy which would qualify me for release from the hospital. Only then did I realize that I couldn't do anything, literally. Even before I progressed back to the point where I could brush my teeth and shave, I had to be taught how to lift something as small as an eight-ounce stick, like a pencil. Then I had to learn how to curl it above me, like a weight-lifter curling his weights. It took a superhuman effort, and only the incentive of knowing I had to do it or I was going to spend the rest of my life in that hospital gave me the strength I needed.

It took four people to move me from my bed into a chair, and the chair wasn't across the room or down the hall — it was right next to my bed.

My therapy began on a Monday morning. The therapists — Chris Downes and Tamerill Faison, whom I called "Tar Heel" because she is from North Carolina — pointed to a set of parallel bars just in front of us and told me, "If you want to go home Friday, you'll have to be able to walk the length of these parallel bars." They were about fifteen feet long.

But the challenge on that Monday morning wasn't to walk that far, it was to walk period. I could not take that first step. I was standing there, with my head down, when the therapists actually had to reach down and lift my left foot and move it forward, taking my first step for me.

Then they asked me, "Why do you have your head down?"

The Value of a Greeting Card

I said, "Because I'm afraid I'll fall backward if I hold it up."

They said, "You're not going to fall backward. We're not standing behind you. We're standing in front of you, because if you're going to fall anywhere, it will be forward. You'll fall flat on your face if you don't lift your head up."

I shocked them by walking the length of the parallel bars that Monday. So they stepped up the goal for me. They said I'd have to be able to walk the length of those bars and back — a round trip — by Friday if I wanted to go home. I shocked them again by making the round trip the next morning, Tuesday.

So then they set another goal beyond the parallel bars that I'd have to reach by Friday. I reached it the next day, Wednesday. On Thursday it was the same story. That's how determined I was to go home. And by Friday, I was ready.

Thirteen
SETTING GOALS AND
MEETING THEM

O n that day, one month and two days after my helicopter touched down on the helipad at Johns Hopkins, I held a news conference in a wheelchair at the hospital to announce I was going home. I didn't do it for the publicity. I did it so I could ask the media to leave me alone for a month while I continued my recuperation at home. To their credit, they did. I thank them for that, because by honoring my request, they helped me to recover.

My doctors were at the news conference with Kathy and all five of our children. I was surprised at how many reporters, photographers and camera crews turned out from every newspaper in Washington and Baltimore and from

217

radio and television stations in both cities.

The atmosphere was one of relief, even jubilation. It was like talking to reporters after winning a big game, and I was on my way to winning the biggest game of my life. It was raining outside, but the sun was shining in that room.

I made sure to thank Kathy and our children and the other members of my family for their unwavering support, everyone who sent messages or gifts, the doctors, and all the other members of the hospital staff for saving me. Then I made special mention of the donor whose liver gave me my new lease on life.

I didn't know the person's identity then, but this much I knew already: Her age didn't make any difference. If you get a healthy liver, and that's the only kind ever involved in a transplant anyhow, the age of the donor is not a factor. I learned that the liver is the only organ in the human body that never ages. So my liver is as healthy — and as young — as anyone else's.

At the news conference, I mentioned the order of priorities which I have emphasized to everyone — our children, my history students, my basketball players and myself — throughout my personal life and my career: God, family, and education in that order. Basketball or anything else can be no higher than fourth. I tell our new players, "If you came to DeMatha because basketball is the most important thing in your life, you're not going to make it here, because your priorities are out of order."

I told the media that my brush with death didn't change my priorities. "After an experience like that, you often hear it said that it is time to re-evaluate priorities. I don't plan to do that. Rather than suggesting a change in these priorities, I believe my illness confirms them."

I finished by saying flatly, "I'll see you on the first day of practice, November 8."

A reporter asked the chief of liver transplantation at Hopkins, Dr. Andrew Klein, if it was realistic to expect me to be able to return to coaching at the start of the new season. Dr. Klein said, "I have every expectation that he will."

Dr. Thuluvath, who was instrumental in saving my life in those first critical days and hours, told the reporters he expected me to make a full recovery within a few months and feel better than I did in the year before my surgery. He was right. That's exactly what happened.

Another reporter reminded the doctors that I was known as a strong, "Lombardi-type" motivator and asked if I might be even more motivated after this experience.

Dr. Klein answered, "He faced the ultimate challenge — death — and motivated himself to overcome it. You couldn't ask for a better motivator than that."

We couldn't leave the hospital until eleven o'clock that night because the staff wanted me to get some more blood to keep building me up. Because it was so late, the staff asked me if I wanted just to spend one more night there and go home the next day instead of having to travel so late at night. I said, "No, no. I don't think so. Thank you."

We drove down I-95 from Baltimore to Hyattsville in Brendan's car, with him at the wheel and Kathy and Joe in the back seat. Over the next few days, I had the pleasure of watching myself on the evening news as the TV stations broadcast the story of my news conference and my departure from the hospital. I could see that I looked a lot thinner — almost dying can do that to you — but the bottom line was that I was still here, and the future looked bright, so bright that I felt confident about meeting my two goals — to be on hand for the first day of practice and to dance at Brendan's wedding eight days later, on November 16.

The reporters must have felt as upbeat as I did. Their stories on TV and radio and in the papers were universally optimistic. One particular headline summed everything up as far as I was concerned. It said:

DeMATHA'S WOOTTEN PROMISES TO RETURN

The Post's award-winning columnist, Thomas Boswell, wrote a column headed:

DEATH-DEFYING WOOTTEN EMERGES LARGER
THAN LIFE

It was all very flattering, but nobody, of course, is larger than life, certainly not me. The thing that mattered to me

*Morgan reaching his second goal: Dancing with
Kathy at their son's wedding.*

was that when basketball practice started three months later, I was there, with my whistle around my neck and ready to go. So were the members of the media. When they honored my request to allow me the time and privacy to complete my recovery after leaving the hospital, I was grateful but not surprised. I have always found the vast majority of the members of the news media to be fully professional and honorable, so I was confident they would leave me alone. They didn't disappoint me.

With that cooperation and privacy, I was able to continue my physical therapy at home, thanks to heroic assistance from Joe, Vince Scalco and Jeff Wright. Jeff is the chief therapist at Providence Hospital. Vince is a long-time DeMatha friend who has sent five sons to our school among his nine children. He and Joe handled my therapy at home, and it's a good thing because Kathy couldn't do it alone.

At home Joe and Vince had to lift me into the shower and other kinds of things that Kathy simply couldn't handle. They drove me to my many physical therapy sessions at Providence Hospital in Washington, lifting me in and out of our car and lowering me ever so gently into my wheelchair and lifting me out of it. They helped me to complete my first complete tour around the first floor of our house with the assistance of a walker and to graduate to a walker with wheels and then to a three-pronged cane. That first complete cycle took me five minutes.

There seemed to be a certain symbolism in that month at home, with all the help I received from Kathy, Joe and Vince. Everywhere I turned, literally, someone was there to help me. It seemed to symbolize everything about my illness and my recovery, from my collapse at Mount Saint Mary's to the present. Every time I needed something — and many times before I even knew I needed it — someone was there for me. From that Sunday until this minute, it seems that the whole world has lifted me up and swept me forward.

At Providence, Jeff told me he was taking personal charge of two patients, James Cardinal Hickey and me. Cardinal Hickey is the Archbishop of the Archdiocese of Washington, who was recovering from heart bypass surgery. As a consultant to Reebok athletic shoes, I kidded him about wearing the wrong brand of sneakers. "Your Eminence," I said, "we have to get you in the right kind of shoes." We did, too. I got him a pair of Reeboks, and he told Jeff to assure me that he was wearing them in his physical therapy sessions.

Everything in my sessions with Jeff was upbeat, just like at Johns Hopkins. He had me thinking I was the strongest man in the world just because I could bench-press ten pounds. When I went up three steps at the end of my first week under his training and supervision, Jeff acted as if I had just won a Gold Medal in the Olympics.

We started basketball practice on November 8 — the

same date every year — and before the month was out, Kathy Orton wrote a feature story in *The Post* calling my presence at DeMatha's first practices of the new season the "rebound of a lifetime." It may not have been the greatest rebound of all time, but I was sure of one thing: It was the greatest rebound of *my* lifetime.

Eight days later I reached my second goal. On November 16, at the wedding reception for Brendan and Elizabeth at a lovely beach club on Long Island, I walked onto the dance floor with Kathy, put my arm around her waist and took the first few dance steps. Everything was infinitely easier than when the therapist had to pick up my left foot and put it in front of me for my first step at the hospital three months before.

The first notes of *The Wind Beneath My Wings* came over the speaker system. As I looked at Kathy and listened to the song, its words held a special meaning in my renewed appreciation for her:

> Did you ever know that you're my hero?
> And everything I'd like to be?
> I can fly higher than an eagle,
> 'Cause you are the wind beneath my wings.

The Wind Beneath My Wings, by Larry Henley and Jeff Silbar
© 1982 Warner House of Music & WB Gold Music Corp.
All Rights Reserved. Used by permission.
Warner Bros. Publications U.S. Inc., Miami, FL 33014

The Wootten Family (from left to right): Mike, Cathy and Nicholas Stamper; Tricia Wootten, Morgan and Kathy Wootten, Brendan and Elizabeth Wootten, Joe Wootten, Bucky, Kiersten, Carol, Stephen and Steve Paul

Fourteen

One of the biggest heroes of all in my case was my donor. Through the organ donor program, I was able to make contact with her husband, Ray McCoy, and express my thanks to him personally for her act in saving my life. He told me his wife was named Rochelle and that she was the young mother of their nine-year-old twins, a son named Ray and a daughter, Randall.

They live in Pasadena, Maryland, between Baltimore and Annapolis, only a half-hour from our home. She was interested in the donor program never dreaming, of course, that she would die suddenly at an early age from a brain aneurysm. She was thirty-three years old. Besides work-

227

ing together to raise the twins, she and Ray also worked at the same place of employment, North Arundel Hospital in Glen Burnie, just outside Baltimore, where Rochelle worked in finance and Ray is in the purchasing department.

Her liver saved my life, and her husband told me that he and the other family members were not surprised to learn from the donor program that I was the recipient of his wife's liver. I had written to the program saying I was anxious to contact my donor's family if they were agreeable, so I could try in some small way to say thank-you for Rochelle's combined act of both heroism and generosity in donating her liver to me.

Members of the donor program staff contacted Ray while I still did not know Rochelle's identity or his. Only a few weeks later, I received a letter from Ray. Not long after, we had a beautiful forty-five minute conversation on the telephone and have since been together on several occasions.

They are sports fans, and when they heard on the evening news that I had been taken critically ill because of liver problems and needed a transplant to save my life, they wondered if Rochelle, who died on the morning of July 9, might be the one who gave me a second life on July 10.

"The day my wife passed away," Ray wrote, "we happened to be watching the news and heard your story on television. Our family found it to be totally coincidental.

*Rochelle McCoy, the woman whose liver saved
Morgan Wootten's life, on her wedding day.*

Therefore, we followed your press conference and the stories published in the newspapers." Ray said later that he saw a clip on the evening news of Kathy saying that our family wanted to thank the family of the organ donor, "whoever they may be." Ray said at that moment, "I got a lump in my throat."

He said the kids could see his reaction and one of them asked, "What is it, Daddy?"

Ray told them, "That gentleman they're talking about on TV may have gotten Mommy's liver."

Rochelle's story proves that you don't have to have a formal signature on a piece of paper to become a donor. The most important step is to make certain your family knows that you wish to be a donor if anything happens to you. In Rochelle's case, it happened because Ray came home after renewing his driver's license in April, only three months before her death, and informed her that he had checked the box saying he wanted to be an organ donor if he were killed in a crash.

Rochelle reacted enthusiastically and told him, "You know, that's a good idea. The next time I renew my license, I'm going to do the same thing." Unfortunately, she never reached that point, but Ray remembered her wishes when she passed away and made them happen.

He was at the hospital with Rochelle's parents, Charles and Shirley Mitchell, and her sister, Nicole Liles, during

Rochelle's final hours, while she was being kept alive by a life support system, a ventilator.

Two parallel dramas were unfolding a few miles apart, involving two families destined to become linked in a common cause to save lives.

Rochelle woke up at four o'clock on Saturday morning, July 6, and told Ray, "I have the worst headache of my life." Only a few hours later, as I enjoyed a Saturday off and prepared to return to our basketball camp at Mount Saint Mary's the next day, Rochelle was in a hospital and undergoing emergency brain surgery.

On Sunday, as she appeared to be making a rapid recovery, I collapsed at camp. That evening, while she enjoyed dinner with her family in her room, I was fighting for my life in the emergency room at Gettysburg Hospital. Then Rochelle suffered a serious setback, and the next day — Monday — both of us were fighting life-or-death struggles. Both families maintained tense corresponding vigils, Rochelle's in the hope that she would improve, mine hoping a liver could be found before I would die.

Tragically, the only thing keeping Rochelle alive was the ventilator. Early Tuesday morning, the doctors told her family she was brain dead. Ray and her parents were faced with that awful decision of whether to keep her alive by artificial means or disconnect the life support system and give her a peaceful death.

They told the doctors to disconnect the ventilator. After Rochelle passed away, Ray and her parents agreed unanimously to donate her organs in response to Rochelle's own stated wishes. If they had not done that, or if, as some families do, they decided to keep her on the ventilator for another few days while they kept hoping against hope, I would have died.

To keep her organs healthy enough to be donated to other patients, the doctors kept her on the ventilator for several more hours after she had been declared brain dead while her organs, including what was to become my new liver, were prepared for transportation to their recipients.

Meanwhile, as Kathy and our children were going through their own emotional struggle in the darkest, most tense hours of my illness, they never dreamed that a woman only a few miles away was about to save my life, after she lost her own.

Later Ray said meeting me, and others, "would prove to my children that to the very end, their mother was willing to give life to someone else." He said it would also "show them that a part of 'Mommy' still lives on." I told Ray that the only way I can repay her is by the way I live the rest of my life.

"It was a tragedy, certainly," Ray said, "but out of it has come some good."

Rochelle's heroism did not end with her noble act of giving a second life to me. She did that six other times as well. Seven of her organs were transplanted into others who, like me, were dying. One of her recipients was a nineteen-year-old boy who received her heart. His system rejected it after three and a half weeks, but by that time her heart had kept him alive long enough for the program to come up with another one which is now functioning normally in the young man.

In what surely must be the ultimate act of charity, Rochelle McCoy saved seven lives. If there isn't a medal of honor for such men and women, there should be.

The United Network for Organ Sharing, whose president is my surgeon, Dr. Burdick, has stark figures on the subject of organ transplants and the growing need for donors. UNOS, headquartered in Richmond, Virginia, says that as of April, 1997, 35,420 patients were registered for kidney transplants alone. Another 16,000 were registered for transplants of other organs — the liver, pancreas, intestines, heart and lung. Tissues can also be donated — eyes, skin, bone, heart valves and tendons.

In contrast, only 19,145 transplants — 10,892 of them involving kidneys — were performed in 1995 at the 281 medical institutions in the United States which operate organ transplant programs. The transplant program obviously is losing ground when the number of patients who are registered to receive organs is so much higher than the number able to be performed in a given year. UNOS

Rochelle McCoy with her husband, Ray, and their 9-year-old twins, Ray and Randall.

adds a new name to its national transplant waiting list every eighteen minutes.

Yet the potential is there for many more patients to have their lives saved through transplants. UNOS points out, for example, that it is possible to transplant approximately twenty-five different organs and tissues, including bone and cartilage, bone marrow, cornea, heart, lung, kidney, liver and pancreas. Age is no barrier. Donors can range in age from newborn infants to senior citizens.

You can declare your willingness to become an organ donor simply by signing a Uniform Organ Donor Card. Medical personnel will still ask the next-of-kin for permission to donate the organ in question, so it is essential for you to tell your family members if you want to be a donor so your wishes will be honored if the occasion arises.

Even with the gap between the number of people registered to donate organs and the much greater number of patients who need them, public support for the idea is growing. Michael Jordan has become involved in the national campaign to encourage people to sign up as future organ donors. The American Medical Association arranged for the distribution of three-quarters of a million brochures to fourteen thousand offices of physicians all over the country.

The singing group of Crosby, Stills and Nash became involved. David Crosby is a liver transplant recipient himself, and on his own initiative he approached the National Council of Local Coalitions, which represents all forty-six local coalitions in the organ transplant field. David generously offered these organizations the opportunity to set up information tables, display posters and signs and distribute donor cards and literature at each of their concerts on their 67-city summer tour in 1996. Before the summer was even over, more than a quarter of a million donor cards had been distributed thanks to Crosby, Stills and Nash.

The Coalition on Donation is also working with the Mickey Mantle Foundation. Together they designed a new national logo with the slogan —

> *Organ & Tissue Donation:*
> *Share your life. Share your decision.*

UNOS expanded its own efforts by providing continuing management and coordination of the national program through its staff resources and space. UNOS members also financed the majority of publicity campaigns in two major phases in conjunction with the Advertising Council and the Jerry & Ketchum Advertising Agency.

The Coalition emphasizes both the need to tell your family you want to donate your organs and the simplicity of it. Even if you haven't gotten around to signing a donor card, as long as your family is aware of your desires your organs can be used to save the lives of other people at the time of your own death. Rochelle McCoy saved my life and six others simply by telling her husband that she liked the idea and was going to sign up the next time she renewed her driver's license. That's all it took. If she hadn't told him in that conversation at home, I would not be here today.

For understandable reasons, Ray McCoy and I have learned as much as we can about this subject and have committed ourselves to devoting as much time and energy as we can to support this life-saving cause. In the process, we have learned that the concept of transplantation has been understood since the beginning of time, but it remained only a dream until the middle of the Twentieth Century, when scientists began to experience their first successes. I owe a particular debt to a man I never heard of, Doctor Thomas Starzl of the University of Colorado Health Sciences Center in Denver, who performed the first successful liver transplant in 1967. It was the first liver transplant in the history of the world, exactly thirty years before my own. By 1970, successful transplantations had been performed on the human pancreas, kidney, liver and heart.

Here are three other positive features we've learned:

- Donating organs does not disfigure the body or change the way the deceased donor looks in a casket.
- Donating organs does not cost the donor's family or estate anything.

♦ All major religions approve of organ and tissue donation and consider it a gift, an act of charity.

For those who may worry about whether it's the right thing to do, and whether God approves of organ transplants, the organ donor people have a ready answer:

"Don't take your organs to heaven. Heaven knows we need them here."

Fifteen
THE ANSWER

On the first day of practice for our 1996-97 basketball season, we did things exactly the same way we always do them, on the first day of the season and every other day. After the players shot around for a few minutes to get loosened up, I took my place at center court in my white DeMatha shirt and blue shorts. I lifted the whistle from around my neck and blew it, and every player made a bee line straight toward me, exactly the way they're supposed to, and formed a semi-circle in front of me.

Then I said exactly the same words I say every year. I was determined to keep everything precisely the same. I told them:

"All right, fellas — we're ready to go again to build another great year at DeMatha High School — great in effort, great in heart, great in desire. And we're going to be just as good on the court as we are in the classroom."

Three weeks later, on November 30, we played the first game of our 1996-97 season, in the first round of the Mid-Atlantic Invitational Tournament at Saint Maria Goretti High School in Hagerstown, Maryland. We were the defending champions. As I walked into the gymnasium, I thought to myself, "I'm really fortunate to be here, to be able to walk into this locker room and kick off this season. The doctors told me maybe I could return to coaching next year, but here I am — this year."

I told our team what I always tell them before important games — we would have to play good defense, and we'd have to make every possession a good one. We won the game, 77-72, over Saint John Neumann of Philadelphia, in the 1,420th basketball game played by the DeMatha varsity basketball team. Two days later we successfully defended our tournament championship by defeating the host school, Goretti, 52-50.

Reporters asked me as the season got underway if I changed anything in my coaching methods. I told them I might spend a little more time sitting down during our games, and I might not holler quite as many instructions to our team out on the floor, but then I told them I couldn't

Photo courtesy of St. Maria Goretti Athletics

Morgan and Joe Wootten coach their first game together after Morgan's liver transplant.

really change everything about the way I coached, not after four decades. I told one reporter, "I couldn't change the habits of forty years even if they gave me all new parts."

Our son, Joe, proved his value again as my assistant by filling in for me in two games when I had medical appointments. He had a perfect season — two wins and no defeats. Joe was DeMatha's acting head coach, working with Neal Murphy, who has been my valued assistant for ten years. Under the leadership provided by Joe and Neal, the Stags defeated two of the public schools in our Prince George's County — High Point and Parkdale.

Joe told me he felt confident and wasn't nervous because he knew our system and me so well. He didn't resort to any motivational speeches or try to copy my style. He just went out and did the job he felt prepared for.

It was a natural transition for Joe. He simply applied what he had learned as a player while at DeMatha and as a freshman walk-on for Maryland University under Coach Gary Williams until he hurt his shoulder. He told me later he wasn't worried over any criticism about being the coach's son, either. He said he had already heard that as a player at DeMatha and knew how to handle it, or ignore it. He used to remind people that we went undefeated in thirty games, so if I was showing any favoritism, it obviously was not hurting our team.

By the time he filled in for me in those two games, Joe

already had two years of coaching under his belt, as the youngest Division I assistant coach in the country at Furman University in South Carolina and then as our freshman coach.

During the season, I passed on to our players some of the lessons I had learned from my experience over the summer. I told them to appreciate every day — the sunrise and sunset, the rebirth of nature in the spring and the beautiful colors of autumn, to be thankful for their families and their friends, and to enjoy every day, one day at a time. And to help them get through any difficult times that may face them, I reminded them of one of the sayings that I've passed on to our DeMatha teams and to all the kids who have passed through our summer camps over the years:

Inch by inch, life's a cinch.
Yard by yard, it's really hard.

We won twenty-seven games and lost only seven, with a coach just getting over an organ transplant and the youngest team in the history of DeMatha. We had two sophomores in our starting lineup, and our sixth man was a freshman. Our worst loss was by six points.

The start of the new season in November 1996 was a time of reflection for me after my transplant. I remembered back to 1956, when John Moylan, Buck Offutt and I all came to DeMatha at the same time, when the school was only ten years old. Forty years later, we were celebrating its fifti-

Bruce Reedy Photography

Coach Morgan Wootten directing the DeMatha Stags.

eth anniversary at the same time I was coming back from my harrowing summer experience.

There were eighteen boys at DeMatha when it opened the year after the end of World War II. When we started the 1996-97 school year, the number was over nine hundred. There were the inevitable changes over that half-century, but certain things remained the same — especially the emphasis on what John Moylan likes to call "character over credentials."

As he told Janet Burkitt, a reporter for the *Capital News Service*, during our anniversary period, "We stress men of integrity and character. And if you don't embrace those qualities, you're out of here."

We still have the coat-and-tie dress code, our students still receive instruction in religion every day in all four of their years at DeMatha, and our students still stand up at the beginning of each school day and recite the Lord's Prayer and the Pledge of Allegiance.

We have won championships in every sport — more than fifty titles in basketball, football and baseball alone — but we also received those Blue Ribbon awards from the U.S. Department of Education in 1984 and again in 1991. By the start of the '96-97 school year, our wind ensemble had been selected as America's top Catholic high school band by the National Catholic Bandmasters Association for fifteen of the past seventeen years under the leadership of our band director, John Mitchell.

As that remarkable '96-'97 basketball season, and that's what it was, unfolded, the Good Lord answered my question, the one I asked Him in the hospital — why my life had been spared. Watching those kids put together a season of success while they were so much younger than our opponents and I was still going through the adjustments which always follow such drastic surgery as an organ transplant, the answer came into sharp focus for me.

God was telling me He wants me to stay here so I can continue to do what He wants all of us to do — to touch people's lives.

Other books by Morgan Wootten

Coaching Basketball Successfully, with Dave Gilbert
DeMatha Offensive Notebook, with Pat Smith
DeMatha Blitz Defense, with Hank Galotta
DeMatha Notebook, with Terry Truax
From Orphans to Champions, with Bill Gilbert

Other books by Bill Gilbert

From Orphans to Champions, with Morgan Wootten
How to Talk to Anyone, Anytime, Anywhere, with Larry King
The Duke of Flatbush, with Duke Snider
Over Here, Over There: The Andrews Sisters and the USO Stars in World War II, with Maxene Andrews
Now Pitching: Bob Feller, with Bob Feller
Real Grass, Real Heroes, with Dom DiMaggio
The Truth of the Matter, with Bert Lance
High School Basketball: How to be a Winner is Every Way, with Joe Gallagher
Five O'clock Lightning, with Tommy Henrich
All These Mornings, with Shirley Povich
Keep Off My Turf, with Mike Curtis
They Call Me the Big E, with Elvin Hayes
Public Relations in Local Government, with contributing authors
This City, This Man: The Cookingham Era in Kansas City
They Also Served: Baseball and the Home Front, 1941-1945